Foreword

This guide aims to make people want to discover a unique and fascinating place, **the island of Tenerife**. At odds with the classic guides, we wanted to share, in pictures, a selection of sites to favour during a trip. This book aims to take its place in your library (physical or virtual) between beautiful books, browsed for their photographs, and conventional guides, consulted for their information.

It is designed by travellers for other travellers, on themes that we like, focusing on beaches, hikes (with maps), built area. It leaves plenty of room for natural spaces conducive to healing and relaxation. It contains information to prepare for your stay, to live it and as a souvenir (while waiting to return). Restaurants, party venues and other services are hardly listed, given their fluctuating nature and the many web resources available.

This guide aims to be:

simple: it focuses on the essentials, with a selection of sites that have caught our full attention and a highlighting of our favourites. If you are staying for a short time, start there.

beautiful: an important place is given to the image, to make you want to go to see or allow you to share your discoveries with your loved ones.

and practical: the visual is designed for pleasant reading and quick browsing, with pictograms and numerous references for easy flip.

Contact Us

The approach to a territory and the territory itself evolve over time. In order to offer you a guide that meets your needs and is as qualitative as possible, please do not hesitate to send us your comments.

We thank you in advance for documenting your remarks, so that we can carefully identify which points are appreciated and which need improvement.

For all contacts, please use the email address: guide-tenerife@destination-terre.com, specifying your first and last name.

Contents

Introduction

Quick overview

Country	Spain
Archipelago	Canary Islands, in the Atlantic Ocean
Community	Autonomous Community of the Canary Islands
Province	Province of Santa Cruz de Tenerife
Capital of the province	Santa Cruz de Tenerife
Name of the island	Tenerife
Area	2'034 km² (about 1/4 of Corsica)
Population	927'993 inhab. (2021)
Density	456 inhab./km²
Official language	Spanish (Castillan)
Government	Unitary parliamentary constitutional monarchy
Geopolitics	EU member as an outermost region
Main religion	Catholicism
Currency	Euro/€
Time zone	UTC ±0 for winter time and UTC+1 for summer time, the same situation as in Great Britain.
Country calling code	34 (from abroad 0034 followed by the 9-digit phone number)
Opening hours	Generally, supermarkets are open 6 days a week, from 9 a.m. to 8 p.m. Small shops close between 1 and 5 p.m. The restaurants serve between 1 and 4 p.m. and between 6 and 11 p.m. Banks are generally closed in the afternoon.
Accommodation	The hotel offer is substantial and you will easily find a rental holiday on sites such as airbnb.com, booking.com and homeexchange.com
Electrical sockets	The sockets are of type C and F (220 V) compatible with European sockets. UK plugs require an adapter. Canadian and US plugs require an adapter equally. A converter may be necessary depending on the type of device to be operated, the voltage not being the same.

Geography

The Canary Archipelago is a constellation of **seven main islands resulting from volcanic activity** and anchored in the Atlantic Ocean, just over a hundred kilometres off the Moroccan coast. According to the most common hypothesis, the islands formed gradually, from west to east, following the movement of a hot spot. Thus, the oldest island - Lanzarote - would have started to shape approximately 20 million years ago, while in contrast, El Hiero would have "only" 1.1 million years. Seismic activity continues, however, and Tenerife, around 12 million years old, last erupted just over a century ago.

The island of Tenerife is the largest of the archipelago. It is the result of multiple upheavals within the framework of which several volcanoes succeeded one another, the first in the south (at the level of Roque Del Conde, the oldest part of the island), then in the Teno massif and finally that of Anaga. A major landslide tear off its top, about 170,000 years ago, leaving a deep gash called Caldeira Las Cañadas. In the middle of it gradually raised the local star, Pico del Teide. With an altitude of 3718 m, it is the highest peak in Spain. The successive eruptions of very varied composition, and age have contributed to the rich landscape of the place.

Occupying the centre of Tenerife, **Teide National Park** is one of the main reasons to come on the island. In addition to its intrinsic beauty, this park is important for the preservation of numerous endemic flora and fauna species. It also protects many testimonies of the geological processes that underlie the evolution of this Spanish archipelago.

Teno is a mountain range located in the north-western region of the island, the peaks there sometimes exceed 1300 m in altitude. The many marked ridges that turn into deep valleys or cliffs are very comparable to the Anaga massif, located at the opposite. The two massifs are the result of a succession of lava flows and then collapse. Over time, erosion has finished drawing the topography as it appears today. Both massifs are recognised as a "rural park" and offer countless opportunities for hiking.

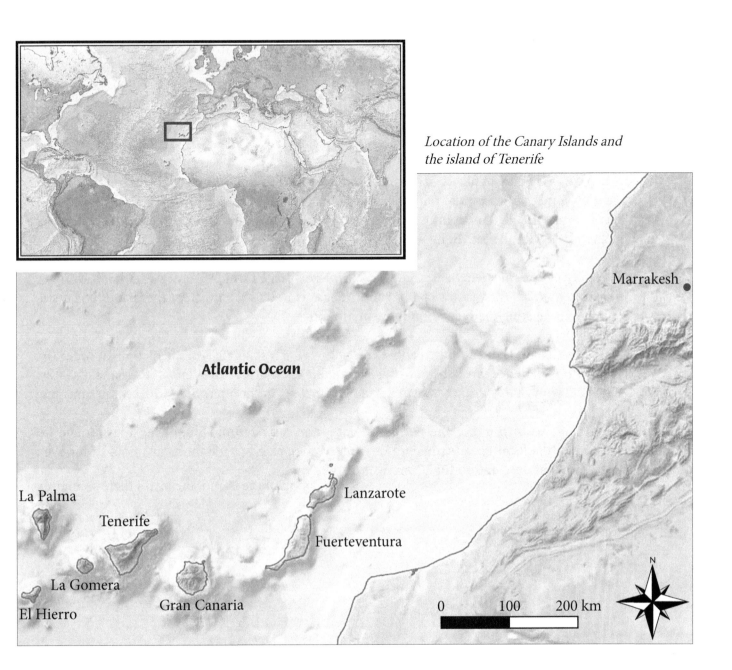

Location of the Canary Islands and the island of Tenerife

Schematically, nowadays, the island is occupied in the north-east by the big cities (the capital Santa Cruz de Tenerife and San Cristóbal de La Laguna), while the tourist infrastructure is concentrated in the south and west, from either side of Playa de las Americas.

Climate

The climate of this island will fill all visitors, its south coast, with mild average temperatures between 18 °C and 25 °C and only 15 days of rainfall a year, or its greener, cooler and windier north coast. The ocean keeps a fairly stable temperature between 19 °C in January and 24°C in the heart of summer, which makes it passable all year round.

The topography of Tenerife generates a number of microclimates which are organized according to altitude and orientation. The massifs of Teno and Anaga, as well as the north of the island in general, capture more rain, making the vegetation more luxuriant.

The Teide National Park is often located above the clouds which stagnate around 1200 m altitude. The daily temperature differences are substantial. For example, the temperature can, on the same day, start at 3 °C with cold wind at daybreak, to warm up and reach 25 °C in the afternoon, with strong sunshine.

When to go there? For swimming, the summer months and early autumn are the most favourable. To take advantage of the local flowers, the end of winter and spring are the most favourable. However, Tenerife is **a pleasant destination for 12 months of the year**.

Tenerife Island

History

The *Guanches*, a people of Berber origin, were probably the first inhabitants of Tenerife. These nomads would so have settled in caves and would have already cultivated cereals 300 years before our era. Isolated, they had developed their own culture and beliefs. The Spanish conquistadors took control of the island in 1496 (after several unsuccessful attempts). The result was dark, many aborigines were reduced to slavery and, even, sent to Spain to be exploited there. Some also succumbed to diseases accidentally imported from the European continent. Imposed Catholicism gradually caused the *Guanches* entity of Tenerife to disappear. Today, Aboriginal folklore is mixed with religious festivals and genetic studies have shown that a significant part of *Guanches* DNA is still present in the inhabitants of Tenerife.

Subsequently, the geographical position of Tenerife contributed to making it a place of important commercial exchange, with the Americas and the Indies. The regular acts of piracy required a continuous presence of the army on the coasts and favoured the urbanisation of small villages on the heights. At the beginning of the 18th century, a period of volcanic jolts, famine threatened the archipelago. Thus, the promise of a better life encourages many families to leave their land for that of the Americas. The dates of the eruptions are not fully known. However, the last one is that of the majestic Chinyero volcano in 1909 (see page 146).

The 20th century, meanwhile, is one of the rise of tourism. At first, people who suffered from health problems such as rheumatism, who came to take advantage of the clean air and the temperate climate to heal themselves. The craze then spread to visitors seeking calm and relaxation. Such was the case for Agatha Christie, who wrote some of her novels while staying at the Gran Hotel Taoro in Puerto de la Cruz. Hotel complexes have grown since then, and some major projects have remained unfinished.

Mobility

Tram in La Laguna.

Coming and getting around in Tenerife

Tenerife has two international airports - Aeropuerto Tenerife Norte (TFN) and Aeropuerto Tenerife Sur (TFS) - which are extremely well served, including by many low-cost airlines.

The coast of the island is well connected with an important bus network, the lines of which also serve destinations with narrow and winding roads such as Masca, in the Teno massif.

The buses are operated by the company TITSA: www.titsa.com (site in English and Spanish).

A tram runs on two lines between La Laguna and Santa Cruz: www.metrotenerife.com (in English and Spanish). For a complete view of public transport timetables, you can use sites like www.moovitapp.com.

The car remains a convenient way to get around Tenerife, especially in the heights.

The highway is free and the roads are in very good condition, even in the mountains.

Many agencies rent vehicles in Tenerife (Avis, Cicar, Enterprise, Europcar, Goldcar, Hertz, Sixt, Thrifty, Topcar...), the conditions of which vary seasonally.

The island is also provided by taxi, white: www.servitaxitenesur.com.

Go from one island to another

Many internal flights to the archipelago allow you to reach the neighbouring islands. The boat is a particularly suitable choice, allowing you to enjoy the trip. Fred Olson (www.fredolsen.es) and Naviera Armas (www.navieraarmas.com) are the main companies serving Tenerife. They also offer a few connections to mainland Spain (Cadiz and Huelva), for those who wish to take the time or travel with their vehicle. Trasmediterranea (www.trasmediterranea.es) supplies some additional maritime connections, in season.

*H*eritage and activities

UNESCO

Two sites are listed as World Heritage by UNESCO, one natural, Teide National Park and the other cultural, San Cristóbal de La Laguna.

The Anaga massif is a UNESCO biosphere reserve.

Museums

The main museums are:

Museo de Naturaleza y Arqueologia (natural history and archaeology, Santa Cruz), Museo Historico Militar de Canarias (military, Santa Cruz), Casa de Los Balcones (history and traditions, La Orotava), TEA Tenerife Espacio de las Artes (arts, Santa Cruz), Fundacion Cristino de Vera (arts, La Laguna), Centro de visitantes Telesforo Bravo (nature, La Orotava), Centro de Visitantes de El Portillo (nature, El Portillo).

Festivities

Unquestionably, the most famous celebration is the **Carnival of Santa Cruz** (www.carnavaldetenerife.com). It is considered to be the second most popular in the world. It takes place over two weeks between the end of February and the beginning of March. Many other festivals (mainly religious) follow one another during the year, in particular:

May	Day of the Holy Cross (Santa Cruz de Tenerife),
May 30	The Day of the Canary Islands, celebrates the autonomy,
May-June	Pilgrimage of Saint Isidore Labrador (Los Real et La Orotava),
July	Pilgrimage of Saint Benito Abad (Saint Cristóbal de La Laguna),
August	San Roque Pilgrimage (Garachico),
	Pilgrimage of San Agustín (Arafo),
	Candelaria festivals,
October 12	National Day.

Excursions and activities

The tourist offer is very extensive and varied. One of the flagship activities is the **observation of cetaceans**, in particular pilot whales (also called pilot whales) and dolphins. Departures at sea take place notably from Los Cristianos, Adeje and Las Galletas, for all budgets, from the small group boat to the private catamaran.

Many other nautical excursions are offered (sailing boats, motor boats, jet skis, kayaks). The coastal waters are ideal for snorkelling and diving. It is possible to find guided outings of all kinds (hiking in the Teide National Park, star gazing, paragliding, cellar visit, gastronomic outing...). The winding roads with sometimes marked drop are appreciated by cyclists.

Some paths to reserve

A definite asset of the island of Tenerife is its many free access hiking trails.

However, there are a few exceptions:

- **Sendero de El Pijaral** (Ananga massif): reservations can be made 15 days in advance. You have to go to the website (centralreservas.tenerife.es/actividad/1) at the earliest in the morning to have a chance of getting a place.
- **Sandero Monte Aguirre** (Ananga Massif): booking can be done 90 days in advance, it is also advisable to book early (www.centralreservas.tenerife.es/actividad/7).
- **Barranco del Infierno** (west coast): by reservation paid access (www.barrancodelinfierno.es).
- **Masca beach** (Teno massif): first free, then closed, the path reopened with a daily quota. You have to book (paying part of the year) here: www.caminobarrancodemasca.com.

We draw your attention to the fact that the conditions of access and the terms of reservation can change quickly. If you would like to use these paths, we advise you to check their status as soon as your arrival date is known.

Access to the Summit of Teide

To get to the top of Teide, you must coordinate the reservation of the cable car (https://www.volcanoteide.com/en/activities/teide_cable_car) with access authorisation. The latter, in great demand, is subject to a daily quota. The steps must thus be carried out as soon as possible, sometimes there is no free place for several months. Weather can interfere. Thus, it is possible to make several reservations, maximum one per week, to improve your chances of reaching the highest point of the island.

The request for authorisation is free and can be done online, here:
https://www.reservasparquesnacionales.es/real/parquesnac/usu/html/detalle-actividad-oapn.aspx?ii=6ENG&cen=2&act=1.
The cable car reservation can be moved or refunded up to 1 hour before departure. Information on daily conditions (weather) should be checked before going there, here is the link:
https://www.volcanoteide.com/en/how-s-the-weather-on-mt-teide-today.

Gastronomy

At the top of the list of agricultural production is the **banana**. Small and sweet, it differs a bit from those normally found (imported) on the European continent. Tomatoes and potatoes are also grown in quantity, while papaya is very visible on the stalls of agricultural markets.

Given the role of the Canary Islands, following the discovery of the Americas, the potato quickly made its appearance and Tenerife has many colourful local varieties. **Papas arrugadas** (or wrinkled potatoes) are a typical accompaniment. These are thin-skinned varieties, cooked in salted water, the salt of which has crystallised on the skin. This accompaniment is often served with **mojo**, a spicy red or green sauce depending on its composition.

The **gofio** is a salted or sweet preparation made from mixtures of grilled cereals, enough to hold in the stomach (a legacy of the *Guanches*).

The proximity to the ocean is also felt in the dishes. Many fish are thus eaten simply grilled. The **parrotfish** (called *vieja*) is a speciality not to be missed.

The **cochino negro canario** (black Canarian pig) is, as its name suggests, a local breed giving high-quality meat.

The production of **goat's cheese** is important, like the quantity of land favourable to goat breeding.

The specific flora of the island allows the production of different varieties of unique **honey**, with several protected designations of origin.

Agricultural markets (mercado del agricultor) are often open on Saturdays and/or Sundays. They allow the direct purchase from local producers. There are notably in Las Chafiras, Granadilla, La Orotava, Tacoronte, Tegueste, La Laguna (municipal mercado).

The municipal market Nuestra Senora de Africa, in Santa Cruz de Tenerife, is renowned for selling the largest selection of fresh (not necessarily local) food.

The microclimates, the volcanic soil as well as prephylloxera grape varieties offer visitors to the Canary Islands and, in particular, Tenerife a rich panel of wines such as the Malvasía, Listan (red and white), Albillo, Verdello... The **vineyard** is subdivided into 5 appellations: Abona, Tacoronte-Acentejo, Valle de Güímar, Valle de La Orotava and Ycoden-Daute-Isora.

Tap water is not always safe to drink and comes from many different sources. It is better to find out locally. Bottled mineral waters are produced on the island: Fonteide and Fuentealta.

*E*conomy

The island's economy is based primarily on **tourism**, followed by agriculture. The cost of living is lower than in France and Great Britain (by 15 to 20%). In the Canary Islands, VAT is replaced by a local consumption tax which varies according to the goods or services. It is, for example, zero on basic products and amounts to 13.5% on alcohol, jewellery and watches. This system of taxation, associated with a strong tourist frequentation, makes that the shops of electronics, watches, perfumes ... flourish. The prices (often negotiable) are, however, not always competitive with your country of origin.

Craftsmanship is underdeveloped and revolves mainly around ceramics, openwork embroidery and basketry.

A tip, 5-10%, is common when service is appreciated in a cafe or restaurant.

*F*auna

Originally, there wasn't any large terrestrial fauna. The **mouflon** is, since its introduction, the most imposing wild animal of the island, where it is present in altitude. Its population is controlled by the authorities to minimise the pressure exerted on the flora. The other species of land mammals are smaller: North African hedgehogs, European rabbits, house mice, rats and shrews.

Half a dozen species of bats are active at night, including the **Canary long-eared bat** (endemic). It is in the water that the presence of mammals is most remarkable. The abysses that surround Tenerife are particularly favourable to cetaceans. Thus nearly thirty species have been counted, the most common of which are the **short-finned pilot whale** (the local star), the common bottlenose dolphin, the Atlantic spotted dolphin and the Bryde's whale.

The winged gent is also well represented, with **more than 300 species of birds** counted. A large part is nevertheless observed only very occasionally (on the sidelines of the usual migratory routes). Ornithology enthusiasts will certainly be interested in the **endemic species**: the Tenerife blue chaffinch, the Canary Islands robin, the Canary Islands chiffchaff, the Berthelot's pipit (also present in Madeira), the Bolle's pigeon, the laurel pigeon and Atlantic canary or simply wild canary (also present in the Azores and Madeira). In addition, there are many local subspecies which could one day be considered as species in their own right (research is in progress). On the coast live many waders (Ruddy turnstone, Eurasian whimbrel...), while boat trips allow you to observe species of seabirds such as Cory's shearwater. Introduced, the Rose-ringed parakeet and the monk parakeet enliven the towns with their cries and bickering.

Also exotic, the only snake on the island is the brahminy blind snake (*Indotyphlops braminus*). It looks like a large earthworm, is harmless and lives in the ground. The other reptiles are mainly represented by several species of **endemic lizards** and by the presence, in the ocean, of a few green and loggerhead **sea turtles**, which are too often disturbed. Two species of frogs take advantage of the rare fresh water points.

Crabs, shrimps, sea slugs and **fishes** enliven the seabed, such as the ornate wrasse, the Mediterranean parrotfish, the Macaronesian sharpnosed puffer (a boxfish), the Canary damsel, the Eastern Atlantic trumpetfish, redlip blenny and fangtooth moray.

Mother and young short-finned pilot whales, one of Tenerife must-sees.

The Tenerife blue chaffinch, a forest endemic species.

The famous wild canary.

Sanderling, a regular shorebird.

Monk Parakeet feeding on Canary Island date palm flowers.

Gallotia galloti eisentrauti, a massive and colourful endemic lizard.

Ornate wrasse, a colourful inhabitant of coastal waters.

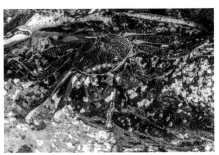

Grapsus adscensionis, a common red or black coloured crab.

Canary red admiral (Vanessa vulcania), a shimmering butterfly.

Flora

The isolation of Tenerife and the entire Canary archipelago has led to the evolution of many endemic species. This is the case for the fauna, but it is mainly the flora which is distinguished by the presence of plants without equivalent elsewhere. In total, **nearly 1,500 species** have been recorded on the island. In particular, various bushy or cactus-like **spurges** illustrate the point well: *Euphorbia canariensis*, *E. lamarckii*, *E. balsamifera* et *E. atropurpurea*.

Some plants form rosettes of leaves that appear to be perched on the end of a stem, such as *Aeonium ciliatum* (a succulent) or *Sonchus canariensis* (resembling a dandelion bush). Others produce noteworthy inflorescences, such as *Canarina canariensis*, with its bell-shaped orange-red flowers, and *Pancratium canariense*, similar to the sea daffodil with its large white flowers.

Less original, the **Canary Island pine** is nonetheless distinguished by its very long needles. It has imposed itself in places and forms an important forest massif, surrounding the Teide National Park. This is the **Corona Forestal** (forest crown), the largest protected area in the Canary Islands, with nearly 47,000 ha.

The island is also home to many species of **viper's bugloss** (*Echium*), including *Echium wildpretii* which adorns the heights with large pink-red inflorescences between late spring and early summer. Another viper's bugloss, *Echium giganteum*, forms bushes that turn white when in full bloom.

Balsam spurge (Euphorbia balsamifera) mainly present near the coast.

Pericallis tussilaginis, a spring flower.

Aeonium urbicum, a succulent with rosette leaves.

Formalities

The formalities for entering the territory are the same as for entering mainland Spain. Thus, for a trip not exceeding 90 days, European citizens, those of the Schengen area, as well as residents from a number of countries such as the UK and Canada do not need a visa.

On the following link, you will find the list of all the other countries concerned and many other useful information: www.schengenvisainfo.com/who-needs-schengen-visa/.

Travel conditions regarding Covid-19 are constantly changing, so it is best to keep informed via the Spanish government website:

www.sanidad.gob.es/en/profesionales/saludPublica/ccayes/alertasActual/nCov/spth.htm.

The following sites are also useful: https://reopen.europa.eu/ and https://travelsafe.spain.info/en/.

Health and precautions

The purpose of this guide is to help the visitor discover interesting places, these, like any destination, are not exempt from risks that can change over time.

Although they decline all responsibility in the event of an accident, the authors should draw the reader's attention to a few known dangers, without proceeding to establish an exhaustive list. Tenerife is not a perilous destination, according to the assessments provided to travellers by several official sites of other countries.

The usual precautions should be taken when **travelling**, bearing in mind that many drivers are on vacation and not used to local traffic conditions.

Natural risks are not excluded, especially in the event of heavy rain. The narrow portions of the barrancos (ravine, dry most of the time) can quickly turn out to be pitfalls with the rising waters. The Canary Islands have experienced several major fire waves. Volcanic activity cannot be completely ruled out, although the last eruption, in Tenerife, dates back more than a century (which is short on the geological scale).

When **swimming** and water sports in general, the strength of the waves and currents (less visible) must be taken into account. Partially submerged cavities can be particularly dangerous.

At altitude, **weather** changes are frequent and can be accompanied by significant drops in temperature. It is therefore advisable to equip yourself both to protect yourself from the sun and from the cold. In general, hiking presents the usual risks (rockfalls, falls, loss of bearings, etc.).

The fauna and flora of Tenerife are not particularly dangerous, it should nevertheless be noted at certain times the presence of **Atlantic man o' war** (*Physalia physalis*). It is a colony of marine organisms similar in appearance to a jellyfish, with a float of 10 to 30 cm and filaments up to 50 m long. These are stinging and can cause a state of shock (with risk of drowning).

Crime is low. However, theft is commonplace. In general, nothing should be left in the vehicles and if possible make the absence of valuables clearly visible (open rear shelf). Breaking into cars (with broken windows) are particularly frequent at the starting points of hikes (Teide National Park, Anaga massif, etc.).
The risks of assault seem mainly linked with night outings (drunk people). However, it appears that several violent robberies have taken place in the south of the island. The authors can testify to this personally. According to information collected from the Guardia Civil (national police forces), it is therefore not advisable to go alone to the isolated areas in the south of the island.

Travel vaccination is an important and complex question that must be anticipated, it varies according to several parameters such as the region, the climate, the season. To prepare for it, here are some links:
- www.healthytravel.ch/home-english/
- www.diplomatie.gouv.fr/fr/conseils-aux-voyageurs/
- www.pasteur.fr/fr/centre-medical/preparer-son-voyage

The **emergency phone number is 112.**

Places to see

*U*ser guide

General Organisation

All the places presented are grouped by region.

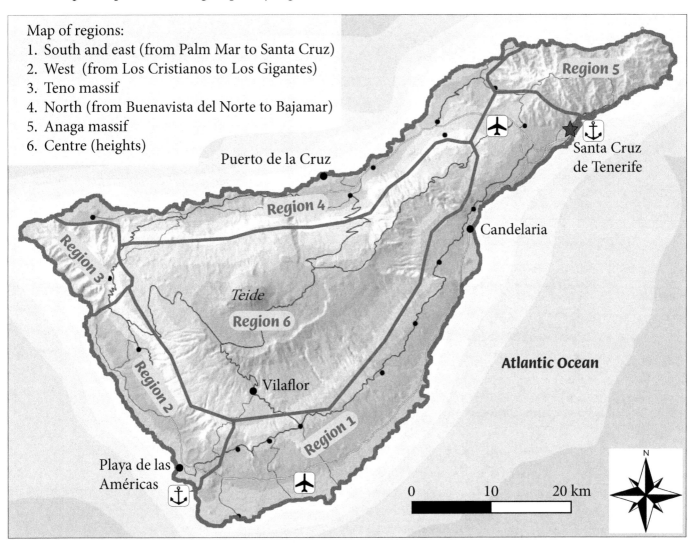

Map of regions:
1. South and east (from Palm Mar to Santa Cruz)
2. West (from Los Cristianos to Los Gigantes)
3. Teno massif
4. North (from Buenavista del Norte to Bajamar)
5. Anaga massif
6. Centre (heights)

Presentation Pages of Places to See

Each place is presented on two pages.

Page number, with region colour.

Place name

The favourites of the authors are indicated. You won't have time to do everything, so why not start there?

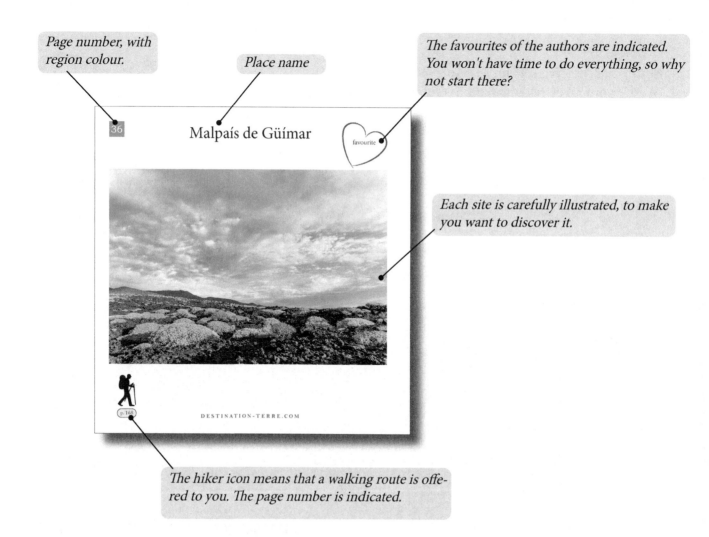

Malpaís de Güímar

favourite

Each site is carefully illustrated, to make you want to discover it.

p. 168

DESTINATION-TERRE.COM

The hiker icon means that a walking route is offered to you. The page number is indicated.

Page number, with region colour.

Place name

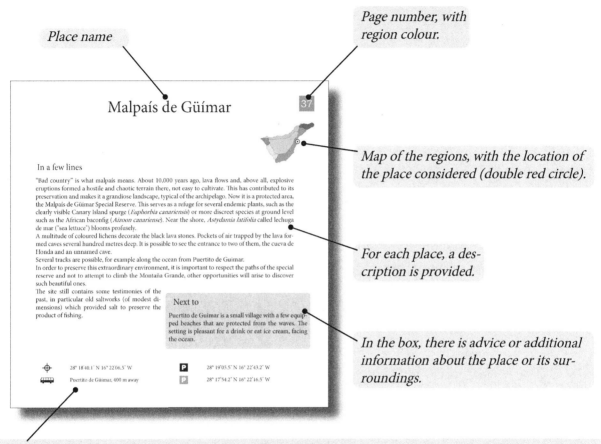

Malpaís de Güímar

37

In a few lines

"Bad country" is what malpaís means. About 10,000 years ago, lava flows and, above all, explosive eruptions formed a hostile and chaotic terrain there, not easy to cultivate. This has contributed to its preservation and makes it a grandiose landscape, typical of the archipelago. Now it is a protected area, the Malpaís de Güímar Special Reserve. This serves as a refuge for several endemic plants, such as the clearly visible Canary Island spurge (*Euphorbia canariensis*) or more discreet species at ground level such as the African baconfig (*Aizoon canariense*). Near the shore, *Astydamia latifolia* called lechuga de mar ("sea lettuce") blooms profusely.

A multitude of coloured lichens decorate the black lava stones. Pockets of air trapped by the lava formed caves several hundred metres deep. It is possible to see the entrance to two of them, the cueva de Honda and an unnamed cave.

Several tracks are possible, for example along the ocean from Puertito de Guimar.

In order to preserve this extraordinary environment, it is important to respect the paths of the special reserve and not to attempt to climb the Montaña Grande, other opportunities will arise to discover such beautiful ones.

The site still contains some testimonies of the past, in particular old saltworks (of modest dimensions) which provided salt to preserve the product of fishing.

Next to
Puertito de Guimar is a small village with a few equipped beaches that are protected from the waves. The setting is pleasant for a drink or eat ice cream, facing the ocean.

Map of the regions, with the location of the place considered (double red circle).

For each place, a description is provided.

In the box, there is advice or additional information about the place or its surroundings.

 28° 18'40.1" N 16° 22'06.5" W   28° 19'05.5" N 16° 22'43.2" W

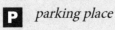 Puertito de Güímar, 400 m away    28° 17'54.2" N 16° 22'16.5" W

Intuitive pictograms provide quick access to essential information.
In order to facilitate the arrival towards the places presented, geographical coordinates are provided. Just copy and paste them into your favourite navigation system, be it GPS, online map (e.g. Google Maps) or smartphone app (e.g. MAPS.ME).

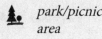 central coordinates of the place

 parking place

 lighthouse

 viewpoint

park/picnic area

 name and distance from the bus stop

other parking options

beach

remarkable tree

Hiking Maps

Each hike is the subject of a map.

To keep you organized, the cards come with the following information:

↔ distance to travel

↗ elevation gain

↘ elevation loss

🕐 estimated walking time

⛰ altitude range in which the hike takes place

The walking time is estimated according to the Swiss Alpine Club standard: one hour for 400 m of ascent, 800 m of descent or 4 km distance. This is the actual travel time, without breaks (change of clothes, route check, etc.).

Page number

Place name

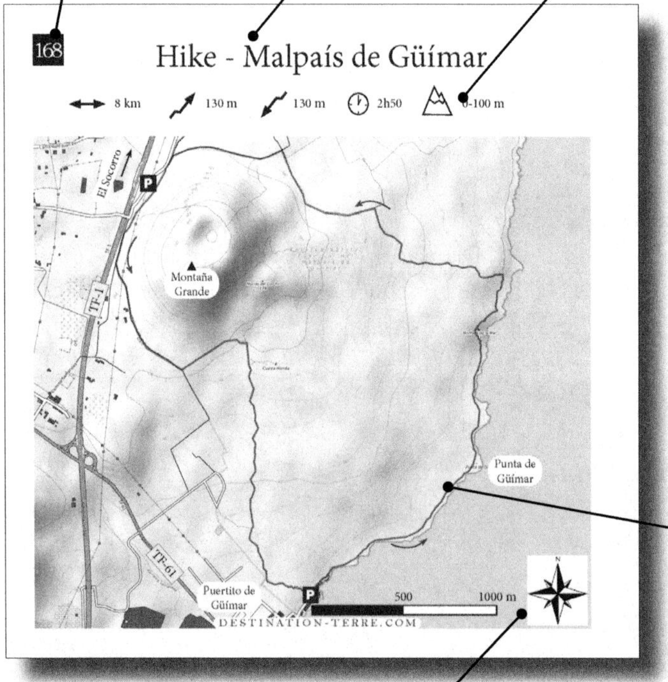

168 Hike - Malpaís de Güímar

↔ 8 km   ↗ 130 m   ↘ 130 m   🕐 2h50   ⛰ 0-100 m

El Socorro
P
Montaña Grande
TF-1
Cueva Honda
Punta de Güímar
TF-61
Puertito de Güímar
P
500   1000 m
DESTINATION-TERRE.COM

The proposed track is shown in blue on the map. The arrows indicate the recommended direction of travel. In some cases, an alternative or an additional section is shown in orange and with a dashed arrow.

Each map is accompanied by a scale bar and the indication of geographic north.

Region 1

South and east (Palm Mar to Santa Cruz)

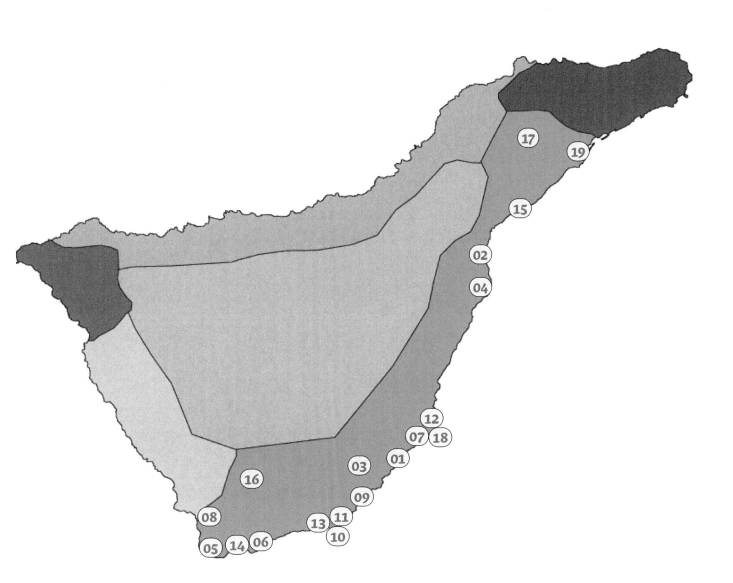

Arco de Tajao

p. 166

DESTINATION-TERRE.COM

Arco de Tajao

In a few lines

The Arco de Tajao is an impressive natural and graphic arch, about 10 m high and 30 m long. This geological formation shaped through the ages can be reached after a short walk from San Miguel de Tajao. For a quick look, it is also possible to stop directly nearby, along the TF-632.

Avoid climbing on it to avoid accelerating the destruction of this work of art slowly sculpted by erosion.

The return on foot is via a shallow and generally dry barranco (a ravine). In case of heavy rain, simply follow the outward path.

If you want to continue walking, you can start from San Miguel de Tajao heading south to reach Las Arenas (a small coastal hamlet). Several beaches and beautiful rock formations will adorn your path. In las Arenas, the Punta de los Surcos is distinguished by a look of lava that seems freshly petrified in the ocean.

The extra advice

The return of the walk is via Cala de Tajao, a small pebble beach, and there are other beaches between San Miguel de Tajao and Las Arenas. So, don't forget the necessary for swimming.

 28°06'56.3" N 16°28'22.3" W

 Tajao

 28°06'36.8" N 16°28'15.1" W

 28°06'32.7" N 16°28'18.1" W

Candelaria

Candelaria

In a few lines

Candelaria is a pretty historic town where, facing the ocean, stand the statues of the nine *Guanches* kings who shared the lands of Tenerife before the Spanish conquest. The village is also known for housing the statue of the Virgin of Candelaria which is located in the cave of San Blas (integrated into the hermitage of the same name). The statue would have appeared in 1392, before the arrival of the conquistadors. A new representation of Mary has been sculpted to replace the original which disappeared during floods in 1826. A feast in honour of the patroness of the Canarians takes place on August 14 and 15, where Aboriginal traditions, folk music and Christian devotion.
In front of the imposing basilica is the main square - plaza de la Patrona de Canarias. From there, calle Obispo Pérez Cáceres offers the possibility to eat something or to go shopping.
Prefer a weekday to discover Candelaria in peace.
When the end of the year celebrations approach, a large nativity scene is erected by the municipality. There, many figurines represent regional history and local life.

The extra advice

South of Candelaria is the small Playa Samarines covered with round pebbles. It's possible to follow the coast (from the Guardia Civil station) to reach it and enjoy a nice view of the city.

		28°20'46.9" N 16°22'08.7" W
	28°21'06.3" N 16°22'11.4" W	28°21'06.3" N 16°22'11.4" W
	Candelaria, 450 m from the basilica	28°21'18.1" N 16°22'11.2" W

Los Derriscaderos

p. 167

DESTINATION-TERRE.COM

Los Derriscaderos

In a few lines

The Los Derriscaderos Natural Monument is a protected landscape in the municipality of Granadilla de Abona (meaning "passion fruit"). It is characterised by a rugged relief, eroded by water, which follows numerous ravines. It is also made of pumice stones cut by the wind. The result is a variety of impressive and visually very attractive shapes.

The proposed hike goes up the main barranco. It is generally dry, with possibly stagnant water in the less exposed hollows. However, it is necessary to take precautions in case of heavy rains.

Along the track, it is possible to observe the remains of past agricultural use (retaining walls, terraces and aqueducts) or modest signs of rock exploitation (galleries). On a clear day, the Teide is also visible during the entire climb.

The place is conducive to the observation of fauna (Berthelot's pipit, Sardinian warbler...) and flora dominated by spurges. In winter, there unfolds a beautiful white flower endemic to the Canary Islands - *Pancratium canariense* - a close relative of the sea daffodil. The more regular supply of water induces that there is more vegetation towards the bottom of the valleys.

The extra advice

The arid barrancos (ravines) of southern Tenerife contrast with the lusher ones to the north. It is therefore advisable to visit one in the north also, to appreciate the differences, for example that of Ruiz (page 98).

28°06'22.5" N 16°30'29.4" W

 28°05'48.5" N 16°30'18.2" W

not served

Malpaís de Güímar

favourite

p. 168

DESTINATION-TERRE.COM

Malpaís de Güímar

In a few lines

"Bad country" is what malpaís means. About 10,000 years ago, lava flows and, above all, explosive eruptions formed a hostile and chaotic terrain there, not easy to cultivate. This has contributed to its preservation and makes it a grandiose landscape, typical of the archipelago. Now it is a protected area, the Malpaís de Güímar Special Reserve. This serves as a refuge for several endemic plants, such as the clearly visible Canary Island spurge (*Euphorbia canariensis*) or more discreet species at ground level such as the African baconfig (*Aizoon canariense*). Near the shore, *Astydamia latifolia* called lechuga de mar ("sea lettuce") blooms profusely.

A multitude of coloured lichens decorate the black lava stones. Pockets of air trapped by the lava formed caves several hundred metres deep. It is possible to see the entrance to two of them, the cueva de Honda and an unnamed cave.

Several tracks are possible, for example along the ocean from Puertito de Guimar.

In order to preserve this extraordinary environment, it is important to respect the paths of the special reserve and not to attempt to climb the Montaña Grande, other opportunities will arise to discover such beautiful ones.

The site still contains some testimonies of the past, in particular old saltworks (of modest dimensions) which provided salt to preserve the product of fishing.

Next to

Puertito de Guimar is a small village with a few equipped beaches that are protected from the waves. The setting is pleasant for a drink or eat ice cream, facing the ocean.

 28°18'40.1" N 16°22'06.5" W

 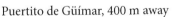 Puertito de Güímar, 400 m away

 28°19'05.5" N 16°22'43.2" W

 28°17'54.2" N 16°22'16.5" W

Malpaís de la Rasca

p. 169

Malpaís de la Rasca

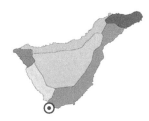

In a few lines

Visible from Montaña de Guaza, Malpaís de la Rasca is formed by lava flows smoothed by time. This nature reserve is home to many species typical of this environment. The first to stand out is undoubtedly the Canary Island spurge (*Euphorbia canariensis*), called cardón.
Lycium intricatum forms modest thorny bushes with slender purplish-pink flowers.
Several birds take advantage of the hiding places provided by bushy plants. In particular, Berthelot's pipit, but also the more discreet spectacled warbler.
Several hikes are possible, following the many paths that crisscross the malpaís. They are sure to amaze visitors. For example, walk along the coast towards the Punta Rasca lighthouse starting from Pal Mar, cross the plateaus of almost black rocks sublimated with mustard yellow lichen and tender green shrubs, then go to the lighthouse. The latter, dating from 1978, is automated. Such was not the case with the tiny old lighthouse, still visible on the roof of the keeper's building, and which required a permanent presence.
The place is also suitable for cycling and, appreciate for fishing.
The Malpaís de la Rasca is recognised for its cultural value, as it still hosts some vestiges of seasonal use by the *Guanches*. The latter were coming there to graze their cattle, to fish, to collect shellfish and to produce sea salt.

The extra advice

With its jagged rocky coasts, the place is conducive to contemplating the setting sun, with a view of La Gomera and its summit clouds.

 28°00'37.9" N 16°41'44.5" W

  Pal Mar, 600 m away

 28°01'16.8" N 16°42'18.4" W

 28°01'33.9" N 16°42'11.6" W

Montaña Amarilla

p. 170

DESTINATION-TERRE.COM

Montaña Amarilla

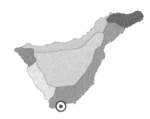

In a few lines

As Montaña Pelada (see page 46), Montaña Amarilla ("yellow mountain") is a natural monument resulting from the underwater volcanic eruption, they nevertheless remain very distinct from each other. It is on the ocean front that Montaña Amarilla stands out, with the succession of warm orange-yellow tones formed by the different layers of rock eroded by winds and tides.

The hike that leads to the ridge reveals a magnificent panorama. A path also circumvents the mountain to the north and allows you to follow a dark and marvellously chiselled coast, dotted with coves within sight, in the distance, Montaña Roja (see page 48).

The sector is home to discrete and endemic fauna and flora, in particular two lizards: the Tenerife gecko (*Tarentola delalandii*), as well as the nominate subspecies of the Tenerife lizard (*Gallotia galloti* ssp. *galloti*).

Costa del Silencio side, at the foot of the mountain is Playa Amarilla, made up of a few natural terraces in the cliffs, not always very stable, and impressive volcanic pebbles. The whole takes on magnificent hues at sunset. Access to the beach is equipped with a few platforms and a small bar, a nice place to relax at the end of the day.

When it comes to swimming, places to bask in the sun are limited and entering the water is quite difficult. However it is a good spot for snorkelling and diving. Abstain if the ocean is rough, because getting out of the water would then be dangerous.

The extra advice

Montaña Amarilla can be bypassed on the ocean side, but only at low tide. Provide shoes with good adhesion and observe the fauna of the puddles (sea slugs, shrimps...).

 28°00'39.5" N 16°38'11.2" W

 Jose Antonio Tavio, 350 m away

 28°00'32.6" N 16°38'19.1" W

 28°00'33.3" N 16°38'23.5" W

Montaña de Abades

p. 171

Montaña de Abades

In a few lines

To discover the Montaña de Abades, you will have to cross the village of the same name. A set of alleys of almost identical white houses, which can be differentiated by the charming way in which certain terraces are laid out. On the seafront you will find several restaurants, a supermarket and ample free parking. From the southern end of it, the path begins in direction to the mountain and runs along a magnificent chiselled coast where small coves of black rocks follow one another. In some places, the terraced topography made it possible, by digging the stone, to create premises for fishermen and also makeshift shelters, probably still occupied today despite the efforts of the authorities.

The shape of the Montaña de Abades gives the impression that a part has collapsed into the ocean. Once at the top, at an altitude of 33 m, a powerful panorama opens up on large dark red cliffs that plunge into the waters. The path leading and skirting the ridge overlooks the void and can be unstable, we recommend being vigilant. The descent furrows on a gentle slope between the euphorbias dressed in their pretty soft green finery (in winter).

The extra advice

Bathing enthusiasts will also be satisfied with two beautiful beaches nearby: Playa de Los Abriguitos and Playa Cardones, north of the village.

 28°08'34.8" N 16°26'18.9" W

 28°08'34.4" N 16°26'12.3" W

 P 28°08'28.4" N 16°26'28.1" W

$\oplus$ 28°08'07.9" N 16°26'35.7" W

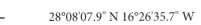 Playa de Abades, 100 m away

Montaña de Guaza

p. 172

Montaña de Guaza

In a few lines

The Guaza Mountain, declared a natural monument in 1994, brings together a number of native plants, endemic reptiles, as well as colonies of seabirds, which require great protection. When they bloomed, low bushes with green-grey foliage of the *Schizogyne sericea* cover themselves with a multitude of small, bright yellow flowers.

Many hiking trails allow you to reach the top of this volcanic cone and enjoy a beautiful view of Los Cristianos, with its hotels and beaches. From Palm Mar, to the south, a path climbs the imposing cliffs that line the coast. It is particularly steep from La Arenita beach. At the top, it offers a breathtaking view of the ocean and, perhaps, of some marine mammals or turtles. To observe common bottlenose dolphins, it is advisable to look (ideally with binoculars) towards the fish breeding ponds.

The area also contains some traces of pre-Hispanic use, old stone quarries, as well as more recent attempts at agricultural cultivation.

The extra advice

In addition to seabirds, the cliffs are home to a very rare species of lizard, so avoid leaving the paths to help preserve this wealth.

 28°02'26.7" N 16°41'40.5" W

 P 28°01'35.2" N 16°42'12.8" W at Palm Mar

 Flamingo at Palm Mar

 P 28°02'36.2" N 16°42'21.7" W at Los Cristianos

Montaña Pelada

p. 173

DESTINATION-TERRE.COM

Montaña Pelada

In a few lines

This natural monument, looking like a crumpled mountain, is the result of an underwater eruption. Here, a lot of fragile ivory-coloured rocks mix with the sand. Thanks to this soil, psammophilous (sand-loving) plants flourish along with bushes of balsam spurge (*Euphorbia balsamifera*). These peculiarities contribute to giving this caldera a lot of attractions and softness.

To discover the beautiful Montaña Pelada, with a diameter of about one kilometre, there are several marked trails. You can go around it or cross the mountain in its centre.
A towel and bathing suit can be useful for enjoying a refreshing stop on Rajita beach, a small jewel hidden in this desert setting.

The surroundings are marked by the will of the authorities of Tenerife for a local supply of energy. Indeed, a solar panel park and a wind farm adjoin this place. It must be said that it is the stronghold of the Instituto Tecnológico y de Energías Renovables, which has the particularity of testing (and renting) bioclimatic dwellings of various and varied shapes (east of the Monaña Pelada).

Next to

Curiosity nearby, an impressive satellite dish, almost 30 m in diameter, rusting, peacefully abandoned at coordinates: 28°03'28.5" N 16°31'40.9" W.
Ideal for those who wish to take a "Mad Max" style detour.

 28°03'48.7" N 16°31'07.8" W

  28°03'43.1" N 16°30'57.5" W

 Playa Montaña Pelada

 28°03'27.5" N 16°31'25.5" W

Montaña Roja

favourite

p. 174

DESTINATION-TERRE.COM

Montaña Roja

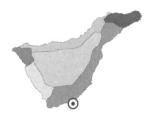

In a few lines

This imposing terracotta-red volcano dominates a coast lined with magnificent beaches. It invites you to explore a protected natural area, as well as superb panoramas. The trails are perfectly marked, you will easily find your way to begin the ascent of this volcanic cone with a high of altitude of 171 m. Slightly to the east of it is the Mirador de la Montaña Bocinegro, a viewpoint that is also very pleasant to look over.

In changing, even gloomy weather, the clearing around Montaña Roja and the play of light between sun and clouds offer very dynamic landscapes that are worth seeing and revisiting.

The sector is also the kingdom of the grey shrike (*Lanius excubitor* ssp. *koenigi*) which watches for its prey, often lizards, from the tops of the bushes.

The extra advice

The place is particularly conducive to marvel from sunset and sunrise. The sun rises year-round over the ocean, while it sets there from late October to early February. The top of the mountain is very busy at certain times of the year. Think about it when you would like to settle there with a good place to enjoy the last light of day.

 28°01'47.9" N 16°32'45.1" W

 28°02'15.5" N 16°32'53.3" W

 Los Balos, 900 m away

 28°02'04.0" N 16°33'10.0" W

Playa del Médano

favourite

Playa del Médano

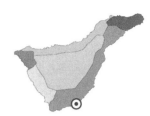

In a few lines

To the north of Montaña Roja is Playa del Médano, a sandy beach wrapped in small dunes and clear rocks that give it a lot of character. It is pleasant to spend time there with the family, the gentle slope makes swimming easier for children and ensures a gradual entry into the water for older people. This spot is known for hosting world kite surfing and windsurfing competitions. Nautical sliding sports have priority. Therefore, reserve swimming for windless periods or do it in the immediate vicinity of the village.

At the southern end, snorkelling, in the middle of the petrified lava and full of cavities, allows you to contemplate myriads of colourful fish (ornate wrasse in particular). On the shore, crevasses are filled with water according to the tide and the wind, you can get there to know some crabs, shrimps or small fish that try to hide when you approach. Sea slugs, also called sea hares, also live there, peacefully eating algae.

The place is popular with waders, birds standing on long legs, like the sanderling or the Eurasian whimbrel.

The extra advice

The surrounding landscape setting is particularly suitable for a yoga session or jogging on the sand, in the calm of the morning.

 28°18'40.1" N 16°22'06.5" W

 28°02'27.5" N 16°32'35.9" W

 Los Balos, 450 m away

 28°02'15.5" N 16°32'53.3" W

Playa Grande

Playa Grande

In a few lines

Playa Grande is located at the foot of the hamlet of Punta de Abona. Integrated in a cove formed in such a way as to naturally protect it from large waves, this beach is attractive for swimming. When it blows, it is ideal for beginning the practice of windsurfing or surfing (depending on the direction of the winds). This superb beach of fine sand, with reflections ranging from beige to black, is especially used by locals who return there for a picnic at the end of the day or on weekends.

The rocks to the east of the beach are particularly good for snorkelling and are also popular with anglers.

The nearby hamlet contains a bar and a few vacation rentals. For other amenities, you will have to turn back to Poris d'Abona, about two kilometres to the north. On Sunday, a modest peasant market (mercadillo del agricultor) opens its doors there.

Next to

About 600 m away is the Faro de Punta de Abona, a lighthouse with the typical red and white colours. The ground is covered with a beautiful black rock, very cut and raw. Beware of the edges which overhang the ocean in places and which can collapse under your feet.

 28°09'09.1" N 16°25'53.7" W

  28°09'08.5" N 16°25'48.4" W

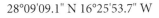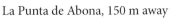 La Punta de Abona, 150 m away

 28°08'53.2" N 16°25'38.7" W

Playa la Tejita

Playa la Tejita

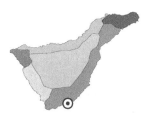

In a few lines

Playa la Tejita forms a huge strip of golden sand about a kilometre long. It is one of the most beautiful, and it's the largest natural sandy beach on the island. It stops at the foot of the Montaña Roja and thus fits into a grandiose panorama. This place is perfect for swimming or just to relax in an incredible setting, but as often on this stretch of the coast, if the wind blows, you will have to leave room for windsurfers.

Nudists are accustomed to settling at the eastern end of the beach. It is risky to go further given the possible collapse of the overhanging cliffs.

Bars and shops are at the other end. In addition to these amenities, there is the rental of deckchairs to the east of the beach.

Near the second car park, a large place is popular for overnight stays in a motorhome.

The extra advice

The sunsets are especially to be observed between November and January, when the beautiful star melts into the ocean. Later, it sets too far north, but remains pleasant to contemplate.

  28°18'40.1" N 16°22'06.5" W

  28°01'59.5" N 16°33'35.3" W

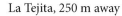 La Tejita, 250 m away

  28°02'03.3" N 16°33'12.6" W

Playa Los Enojados

Playa Los Enojados

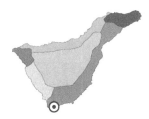

In a few lines

Near the beaches of las Galletas, after the port in a westerly direction, there is a small confidential and charming beach, Playa los Enojades. This modest strip of sand is the most pleasant for swimming in the direct vicinity of Las Galletas and the Costa del Silencio.

Walkers and riders use the path that extends to Punta de la Rasca. Fishermen (on foot) appreciate the indented coasts of the surroundings, while wild camping is practised there from time to time.

Birds, such as grey shrike and Bertholet's pipit, can be observed in the malpaís behind.

The place is nice to enjoy the sunset.

It offers a nice view of the captaincy of Las Galletas, a blue construction with a singular look.

The village of las Galletas, just next door, has all the necessary amenities including play areas for children. It hosts a modest church, the Parroquia san Casiano, original with its two bell towers and its balcony.

From the marina, excursion boats depart to discover pilot whales and other cetaceans.

Next to

At the port of Las Galletas, local fishermen sell their catches in the morning, in a small market. A necessary to taste, the parrotfish called "vieja" (old woman), a Canarian speciality.

 28°00'31.2" N 16°39'48.7" W

 28°00'33.8" N 16°39'44.4" W

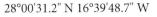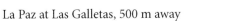 La Paz at Las Galletas, 500 m away

 28°00'30.7" N 16°39'29.1" W

Radazul

Radazul

In a few lines

With land reclaimed from the cliffs and the ocean, Radazul is very man-made. It therefore denotes with the places presented in the previous pages.

The locus provides easy access to the water with its beach set in an imposing sea wall, which particularly attracts divers, who can easily engage backwards in the water.

From the end of the car park, heading west, a path runs along the cliffs and offers a lovely view of the coast as far as Guimar. It joins Playa Tabaiba in the village of the same name. On the other side, Playa de Radazul is followed by the marina, then, further east, by a park and a large playground. Next is Playa de la Nea, a long beach covered in black sand about 300 m long.

The extra advice

If you want to enjoy the pleasures of Radazul, come early, because the car park fills up quickly, especially on weekends!

28°24'06.0" N 16°19'33.0" W

28°24'14.3" N 16°19'06.0" W

 28°24'06.3" N 16°19'28.5" W

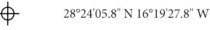 28°24'05.8" N 16°19'27.8" W

 Radazul, 50 m away

Roque de Jama

DESTINATION-TERRE.COM

Roque de Jama

In a few lines

The Roque de Jama (also called Roque de San Miguel) is a remnant of the Adeje massif, resulting in the formation of the first shield volcano at the origin of Tenerife. Its singular shape suggests millions of years of erosion where only the strongest rocks have held out. The ascent of the castling promises some strong sensations, first of all, by skirting a vertiginous wall, then by reaching the summit where a marvellous panorama opens up covering the south of the island.
It also allows you to admire the surrounding terraced crops.
An endemic lavender (*Lavandula canariensis*) punctuates the rise with purple spots, while spurges and sow thistles add a touch of green and Indian fig opuntia pear adds a bit of prickliness.
In the air, with a bit of luck, the peregrine falcon will fly towards the cliffs.

Next to

The Mirador de la Centinela gives access to a panorama comparable to the view from Roque de Jama. This stone-built platform has a bus stop and parking spaces.

 28°04'41.7" N 16°38'22.4" W

 28°18'40.1" N 16°22'06.5" W

 28°05'42.5" N 16°38'27.7" W (few places)

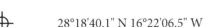 El Llanito, 600 m away

 28°05'33.3" N 16°38'07.5" W

San Cristóbal de La Laguna

San Cristóbal de La Laguna

In a few lines

Known more familiarly as La Laguna, this small town saw its construction begin at the end of the 15th century, on a large plateau at the level of a big lake from which its name derives. Then it extended further south according to a chequerboard architecture. The first city to abandon the fortifications for modernity, it will be an example for the future cities of South America. La Laguna is home to a number of religious buildings and beautiful colonial houses, which has earned it the status of UNESCO World Heritage Site since 1999.

It was the first capital of Tenerife, until 1823, before Santa Cruz de Tenerife took this title from it after a marked growth around the port area.

Discovering the Laguna means strolling through the streets of the historic centre and admiring the colourful houses, decorated doors and windows, of the colonial type. It is also an opportunity to taste churros accompanied by their hot chocolate.

Two religious buildings deserve a detour, the cathedral of Nuestra Señora de los Remedios, one of the major places of worship in the Canary Islands, and the church of the Immaculate Conception, dean of the archipelago.

The Plaza del Adelantado, an important living space for the inhabitants of San Cristobal, has seen many festivals, markets and even executions over the centuries.

The extra advice

In town, you can observe some beautiful examples of the emblematic Canary Islands dragon tree, especially near the cathedral, the Plazoleta de Zerolo and the Plaza de la Junta Suprema de Canarias.

    28°29'21.4" N 16°19'05.2" W

 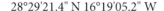   Intercambiador Laguna

    28°29'17.6" N 16°18'45.7" W

    28°29'11.6" N 16°18'44.9" W (paying)

Sanatorio de Abona

Sanatorio de Abona

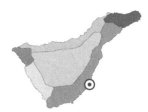

In a few lines

Medicine has progressed faster than expected. Antibiotic treatments allowed to keep the sick at home. Thus the Sanatorio de Abona, a major leprosarium project of the 1950s, was abandoned. The constructions have remained unfinished and neglected for about 70 years. The complex is impressive, a sensation reinforced by its isolation. It is overlooked by an unusually sober church, made of concrete brick, like the other buildings.
A real little ghost town used temporarily, in the 80s, for military exercises.
Several artists have left their mark on the walls. Varied graffiti, some of which stand out for the finesse of their lines or the originality of the subject.
Despite the prohibited entry, the site is sometimes very busy.

The extra advice

Entrance to the buildings of the Sanatorio de Abades is prohibited due to the risk of collapse. Moreover, it is private property. The decision to visit it from the inside will therefore be at your own risk. If you choose not to enter, you can still see the constructions from the outside.

 28°08'46.5" N 16°26'13.2" W

 28°09'08.7" N 16°25'48.3" W

 Abades, 400 m away

 28°08'30.5" N 16°26'26.2" W

Santa Cruz de Tenerife

Santa Cruz de Tenerife

In a few lines

Santa Cruz de Tenerife is known worldwide for hosting one of the biggest carnivals and, on a smaller scale, for being the capital of the island of Tenerife. Its economy depends largely on tourism, but also on important port activity due to its strategic position in the Atlantic. Its very varied architecture allows you to appreciate the contemporary curves of the Auditorium of Santa Cruz Tenerife or historical monuments such as the Church of the Immaculate Conception dating from the 16th century. The neighbourhoods around this church are among the most interesting. It is also pleasant to go for a walk in the landscaped park of García Sanabria. This well-maintained place has many plants, with a sand-filled children's playground, a pond fulled of Perez's frogs and a few vagrant terrapins.

There's something for everyone in Santa Cruz: fresh produce at the Nuestra Señora de África market, the souvenir photo at the Spanish Square, the particular appearance of the fig trees in front of the church of St. Francis of Assisi, the International Party and Congress Center of Tenerife, the Tenerife Arts Centre (TEA, building designed by Herzog & de Meuron), shopping everywhere (encouraged by low taxes)...

Next to

To the south of the city, an old landfill has been rehabilitated to house the Palmetum de Santa à Cruz. The paid entrance gives access to a park adorned with many palm trees from around the world, as well as a varied endemic flora, all carefully laid out and ordered by continent.

  28°28'19.9" N 16°15'13.8" W

  28°27'36.0" N 16°14'57.5" W

28°27'53.5" N 16°15'05.8" W

 28°27'17.4" N 16°15'16.8" W

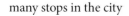 many stops in the city

Region 2

West (Los Cristianos to Los Gigantes)

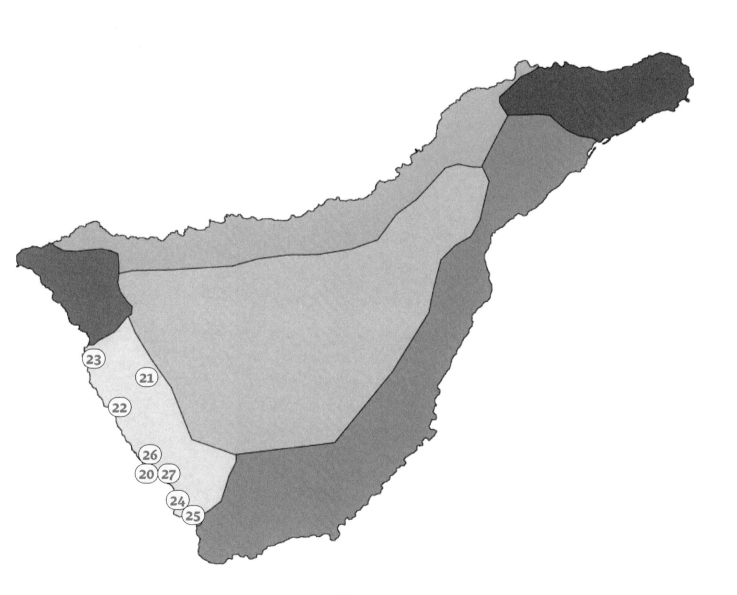

La Caleta de Adeje

favourite

La Caleta de Adeje

In a few lines

This natural beach, also called Playa Diego Hernández, is part of the "La Caleta" site of scientific interest. Sandy, it is about 200 m long. Its gentle slope is ideal for children and for water games. Impressive cliffs are an extension of the beach to the south, while to the north-west more modest cliffs also provide cachet.

To reach the shore, you have to follow a path along the golf course, in the vegetation and small pebbles, for a distance of nearly 800 m. Good shoes are therefore useful. The flora is a little hostile (mainly due to the presence of Indian fig opuntia, with their prickles). This is the price to pay to benefit from a still wild site at the foot of sumptuous cliffs.

From the bus stop, the walk is longer. You have to follow the hiking path that goes up between the buildings located at the end of Playa de Diego Hernández Street (28°06'14.3" N 16°45'21.5" W).

There is no service. Drinks are sometimes sold by users of the beach.

Attendance is quite heterogeneous, partly without textiles, with a relaxed and friendly atmosphere.

The extra advice

This is a very good location to admire the sunset, on the ocean or behind La Gomera, depending on the season.

 28°06'30.8" N 16°45'40.5" W

 La Caleta de Adeje, 1.6 km away

 28°06'42.7" N 16°45'19.0" W

Guia de Isora

Guia de Isora

In a few lines

Guia de Isora is a modest town with typical Canarian architecture, the small streets, the colourful facades and the roof terraces set the tone. No one entrance looks like the next, due to the varying hues adorning the doors and shutters.
Here, there is life and sunshine! In the centre, the beautiful church of Nuestra Señora de la Luz is a pleasant discovery. From there, the streets Abajo, de Arriba and La Vera are the most attractive. It is precisely along the Vera that there is a confectionery dating from 1905, which perpetuates an ancestral knowledge.

5 minutes from Guia de Isora is the hamlet of Chirche, also well preserved, it has kept all its picturesque charm. Several traditional houses are converted into tourist accommodation and will not fail to satisfy those who would like to get away from the very popular coasts. On the weekend around mid-July, the day of tradition is an opportunity to revive an ancestral way of life.

Next to

The Mirador de Chirche offers a breathtaking view of the surroundings. It is 3 minutes by car from the centre of Church and 650 m on foot, with 110 m of elevation gain.

 28°13'16.6" N 16°45'34.3" W

 28°12'38.4" N 16°46'53.5" W

 28°12'36.5" N 16°46'36.5" W

⊕ 28°12'34.5" N 16°46'44.6" W

 Correos, 200 m from the centre

Playa Abama

Playa Abama

In a few lines

This creek set between the cliffs hosts a large hotel complex, which explains the quality of the services. With the particularity of having a funicular and a small electric train for customer access. Notwithstanding, soft sand (artificial beach), calm waters, surveillance, restaurant and showers are available to all. The walk is about 650 m from the car park and 100 m of elevation, following the road and a banana plantation, then taking the stairs.

At the end of the cove, a dyke breaks the effect of the waves, provides a sheltered area suitable for swimming at all times. However, in strong westerly winds, the light sand may spoil the visit somewhat. A landscaped path leads to a quay and allows a look at the cliffs.

A few fish seem accustomed to being fed by visitors and redlip blenny (Ophioblennius atlanticus) inhabit the waters near the sea dyke.

The extra advice

At the top of the stairs, a panoramic square overlooks the ocean, a suitable place to enjoy the setting sun and admire the coming and going of the waves.

 28°18'40.1" N 16°22'06.5" W

 Abama, 900 m away

 28°10'19.2" N 16°47'54.6" W

Playa de la Arena

Playa de la Arena

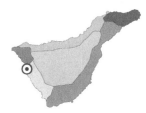

In a few lines

This friendly black sand beach is bordered by rocks of a similar hue, which gives it character. While relaxing there at the end of the day, you can observe the colours of the sea giving way to those of the city of La Arena.

In the extension of the shore, a layout in bleachers is appreciable to settle down and watch the surfers and, above all, the bodyboarders in the waves. The latter can also make access to water tricky, depending on their orientation.

The nearby street front offers a range of shops and services.

Further north is the Playa de Los Guios also called Playa de Los Gigantes, it is located at the foot of the eponymous cliffs and allows you to enjoy their imposing beauty. It is better exposed in the afternoon and quite reduced at high tide.

Next to

Stop at the Mirador Archipenque and enjoy stunning views of the Los Gigantes cliffs.

 28°14'25.3" N 16°50'13.1" W

 28°13'49.2" N 16°50'26.1" W

28°13'49.2" N 16°50'26.1" W

 Playa de la Arena

 28°14'46.5" N 16°50'33.6" W (Playa de los Guios)

Playa de Las Américas

Playa de Las Américas

In a few lines

Originally a beach, now Playa de las Américas is the tourist hot spot in Tenerife. Very popular, the place has been gradually conquered by the urbanisation that extends to the east with Los Cristianos and to the north with Costa Adeje and finally La Caleta.

Made up of hotels, bars, restaurants, shops and close to several amusement parks, Playa de las Américas is also at the heart of the region's nightlife and festive scene.

Located to the west of the city, the beach welcomes surfers, sometimes in large numbers, which does not make it an ideal place for swimming. A barrier of rocks creates a small pool of salt water, suitable for games for the youngest.

From the beach in a southerly direction begins the Francisco Andrade Fumero Promenade, which is very popular, especially in the evening. It borders few hotels with neat architecture.

Next to

In addition to the beaches listed on the following pages, the surroundings of Playa de Las Américas include several large man-made beaches: Playa del Camisón, Playas de Troya and Playa El Bobo.

 28°03'27.4" N 16°43'54.0" W

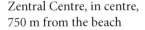 Zentral Centre, in centre, 750 m from the beach

 28°03'32.4" N 16°44'07.5" W (beach)

 28°03'27.4" N 16°43'54.0" W (centre)

Playa de las Vistas

Playa de las Vistas

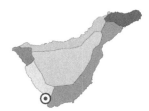

In a few lines

On the coastline of Los Cristianos is the largest man-made beach in the south of Tenerife, stretching over 850 m in length at the foot of Montaña Chayofita. Slightly further east is its little sister, Playa de Los Cristianos, which is more quickly in the shade at the end of the day.

They both offer the advantages of tourist beaches: well-maintained, fine sand, deckchairs and parasols, reduced mobility access, showers, toilets, etc.

On the seafront promenade, restaurants, shops and supermarkets complete this lively place. Several shops diversify the range of services, offering the rental of equipment for water sports.

The extra advice

Playa Vista has the "Blue Flag", a European label which rewards environmental and tourism management.

 28°03'07.6" N 16°43'24.5" W

 28°03'10.1" N 16°43'23.9" W

 El Camisón, 700 m away

 28°02'57.0" N 16°43'13.0" W

Playa el Puertito

Playa el Puertito

In a few lines

The small port at the end of the road, El Puertito de Adeje, is a haven of peace made up of a beach, as well as calm waters full of fish that invite you to put on fins.

The place also hosts a bar which ends up creating a pleasant atmosphere. To the south, one can travel further along the Cala de las Tortugas to arrive at subtle rock formations named Primera Playa Salvaje. A ladder gives access to the ocean (the ascent can be tricky).

Sheltered cove, El Puertito de Adeje is also popular for anchoring boats, stay alert while swimming and, even more, for snorkelling. The proximity of the cliff is the best place to observe schools of dreamfish (*Sarpa salpa*), Mediterranean parrotfish (*Sparisoma cretense*) and Atlantic trumpetfish (*Aulostomus strigosus*).

The extra advice

It was a place famous for the presence of sea turtles. They have however deserted it, following an excess of attention. If you are lucky enough to see one, give it some space, for its peace and the happiness of other observers.

 28°18'40.1" N 16°22'06.5" W   28°19'05.5" N 16°22'43.2" W

 not served   28°17'54.2" N 16°22'16.5" W

Playa de los Morteros

Playa de los Morteros

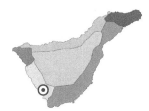

In a few lines

This small cove bordered by a coast that becomes accessible with the tides and whose colours vary subtly depending on the light is less suitable for swimming (difficult access to water) than for contemplating a magnificent coastal landscape. Along the coast to the north, a path overlooking the ocean leads to Caleta de Adeje (page 70).

Like other places in the south of Tenerife, cavities dug into the rock sometimes welcome makeshift travellers. The surrounding vegetation is largely dominated by spurges.

To access los Morteros, follow the hiking path that climbs between the buildings at the end of Playa de Diego Hernández Street (28°06'14.3" N 16°45'21.5" W).

The extra advice

Take your towels and bathing suit, you can stop at La Caleta (the village), further south. There, access to the ocean is easier and there are also all the tourist amenities.

  28°06'18.9" N 16°45'29.3" W

  28°06'16.9" N 16°45'15.8" W

  La Caleta de Adeje, 900 m away

  28°06'08.1" N 16°45'23.3" W

Region 3

Teno massif

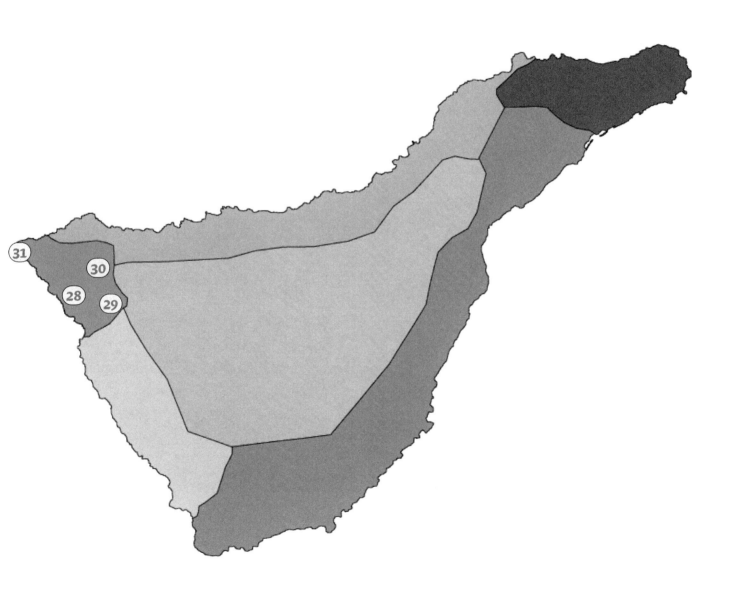

Masca-Roque de la Fortaleza

favourite

p. 176

DESTINATION-TERRE.COM

Masca-Roque de la Fortaleza

In a few lines

The adventure to go to Roque de la Fortaleza begins at the Mirador de la Cruz de Hilda, from where there is an incredible view of the Masca village and its valley. The hike crosses a natural space that looks like a botanical garden. Sometimes uneven path requires special vigilance and the void can put people who are sensitive to vertigo at fault. The place is therefore reserved for good walkers. It is advisable to take it in dry weather. However, the scenery is definitely worth the effort. The omnipresent vegetation green is quite disconcerting and distorts the perception of distances. Emotion and pleasure are felt at every step. Very sloping stone walls have been adapted to allow climbing along certain cliffs, this ingenious design leaves you speechless. What amazing work here in the middle of nowhere! Once the end of the path is reached, old agricultural terraces offer a magnificent panorama, including on the beach of Masca.

The path passes between spurges with large purple inflorescences (*Euphorbia atropurpurea*).

There are few parking spaces and a narrow road in places, so the bus from Santiago del Teide is a good option.

Regarding access to the barranco and Masca beach, see the chapter on booking paths in the introduction (page 15).

The extra advice

Keep your eyes peeled, the Tenerife robin (*Erithacus superbus*), the Barbary partridge (*Alectoris barbara*) and other birds are to be observed along the way.

 28°17'54.3" N 16°51'39.4" W

 Cruz de Hilda **P** 28°18'48.4" N 16°50'44.8" W

Montaña Bilma

p. 177

DESTINATION-TERRE.COM

Montaña Bilma

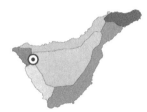

In a few lines

Going around Montaña Bilma (also called Montaña Negra) is the opportunity to stepping on coloured volcanic granules and petrified lava plateaus. It is between the end of January and the beginning of March that the place has the most charm, thanks to the many almond trees then in bloom. The panorama along the route is very diversified. It offers great clearance over the region, the Teide or even La Gomera in the distance. The proposed route passes through closed paths (but practicable and practised) for lack of an alternative to make a loop. However, a variant is proposed. It involves getting off at Santiago del Teide and taking the bus there (or making Santiago the starting point and starting with the bus ride).

Many *Aeonium urbicum* grow on both sides of the path. These are endemic grassy plants which have the particularity of forming rosettes of leaves perched on a stem reaching one metre in height.

Next to

Santiago del Teide is a small village with a charming church. It is a good starting point for exploring the Teno Massif region.

 28°17'36.8" N 16°47'29.5" W

 San Isidro Las Manchas   28°17'06.5" N 16°48'10.8" W

Monte del Agua-Erjos

p. 178

Monte del Agua-Erjos

In a few lines

The north of Tenerife is swept by winds which bring clouds which remain stuck and generously sprinkle the Teno massif. Thus, beautiful green and mossy forests began to develop there about 5 to 6 million years ago, after the exhaustion of an intense period of volcanic activity. These laurisilva (humid subtropical laurel forest) are veritable green relics and Monte de Agua is a prime stopover for discovering them. Once under the canopy, the characteristic plant species are offered to the visitor's eyes. On the ground *Pericallis echinata* forms pretty purple flowers at the beginning of spring. Tree heather, which blooms at the same time, occupy an important place in the understory.
It is also an appropriate place to discover Bolle's and laurel pigeons, two endemic birds, unless you only hear their cooing and flapping wings in the canopy.
This location provides a striking contrast to the many arid places offered by the island of Tenerife.

The extra advice

The forest is humid and cool, think about it during your preparations. Once there, take the time to marvel at the rich flora that a single tree can accommodate (moss, lichens, mushrooms and other epiphytes).

$\oplus$ 28°19'40.0" N 16°48'40.5" W

  Erjos, 150 m away   **P** 28°19'42.1" N 16°48'21.2" W

Punta et faro de Teno

Punta et faro de Teno

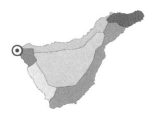

In a few lines

The wild and vertiginous landscapes, crossed to reach the Punta de Teno, give the feeling of having arrived at the end of the world! The access road had also collapsed in 2016, contributing to a certain isolation.

This point is a great location to appreciate all the presence of the cliffs of Los Gigantes. These giants extend along the northwest coast of the Teno Natural Park, over a length of 12 kilometres. While their height varies between 300 m and 600 m. The submerged part of the cliffs and the low accessibility favour the richness of the marine ecosystem. The topography is very marked, alternating between cliffs and deep narrow valleys, the best known of which leads to the beach of Masca.

Arrived at the tip of Teno, the site is discovered by taking a path laid out in wood which slips between the rocks and reveals superb landscapes. The lighthouse can only be seen from afar, its access being closed.

From this sector, trails run along the coast, towards the south, where you have to climb, or towards the north, towards Punta Gorda. The surroundings are home to a high density of Tenerife lizards (*Gallotia galloti*) and Tenerife geckos (*Tarentola delalandii*). As well as small beaches covered with volcanic "pebbles", which actually look more like cannonballs.

Access by private vehicle is sometimes limited. Several variants of timetables followed one another to encourage the use of public transport. It is therefore advisable to find out about the latest timetables before going there and to favour the bus (see chapter on mobility, page 13).

Next to

Stop at the Mirador de la Punta del Fraile and admire the view of the wild coast of northern Tenerife interspersed with the famous banana plantations! Watch out for falling rocks.

 28°20'30.0" N 16°55'15.1" W

 28°22'01.0" N 16°53'04.1" W

 Punta de Teno, 100 m away

 28°20'35.5" N 16°55'11.6" W

Region 4

North (Buenavista del Norte to Bajamar)

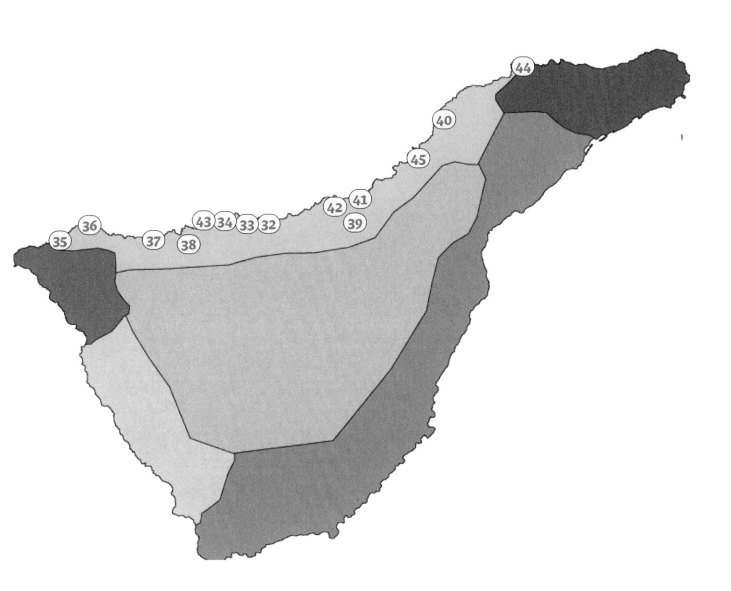

Barranco de Ruiz

p. 179

Barranco de Ruiz

In a few lines

This is a special protected area, as it is covered with vegetation typical of the northern coastal areas of Tenerife. Very green, this barranco is flared and deep. A landscaped path goes up it, before reaching a small square called Pedro Dominguez. In the centre of it sits a Canary Islands dragon tree around which are organised a few benches suitable for a well-deserved break. From this place, the view of the barranco and the surroundings are very pleasant.

From there, the hike continues towards Lavaderos de la Vera, an old wash house with a lot of charm. Another option for a stopover, more refreshing and shady. Then, further on, a spring offers itself to the visitor, in a dense understory.

On a portion of the western flank of the ravine, a succession of terraces bear witness to past agricultural exploitation, which has fallen into disuse. Barranco de Ruiz now serves as a refuge for fauna and flora. It is a place suitable for bird-watching: wild canary, Barbary partridge, peregrine falcon, Bolle's pigeon...

Echium giganteum, called tajinaste gigante, forms spectacular bushes covered with white inflorescences. While the tree aeonium (*Aeonium arboreum*) tries to steal the show with its large yellow inflorescences.

The extra advice

Practise this hike at the end of winter to enjoy a little flowering vegetation and, with some luck, spectacular views of the Teide covered with its white mantle.

28°23'10.9" N 16°37'38.5" W

Barranco de Ruiz

 28°23'28.9" N 16°37'35.4" W

Charco De La Laja

Charco De La Laja

In a few lines

Magnificent natural pool, one of the most beautiful in Tenerife! Plans to go there at low tide and in calm weather to swim there. If, on the contrary, the weather is rough, we admire the show of the waves crashing there and thus feel all the power of the ocean. This place has easy access (stairs) and comfortable, everything has been laid out in stone slabs and the whole fits perfectly with the charco.

Further west, and less known, are the charcos Verde and de la Arena, very discreet within steep rocks. They can be admired from above, access to the water being reserved for the intrepid (and for fishermen).

Next to

A few steps away is the Playa de Los Roques, as its name suggests there is an impressive rocky islet. This beach is particularly photogenic (but not suitable for swimming)! Also enjoy visiting the centre of San Ruan de la Rambla, the square around its church.

 28°23'51.9" N 16°38'41.9" W (Pl. de los Roques)

 28°24'01.6" N 16°39'29.9" W (Verde et Arena)

 28°23'46.7" N 16°39'06.5" W

 28°23'37.9" N 16°39'05.9" W

 Los Palomos, 300 m away

Charco del Viento

Charco del Viento

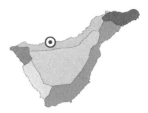

In a few lines

The access path begins right at the car park, suddenly the view of the basin formed by jagged lava is exceptional, really some Charco that has appearance. Three small narrow beaches have formed according to the comings and goings of the waves. Prefer the pool on the left when you come, the waters are calmer there, because the entrance is closed with rocks. The road to reach this charco crosses the banana plantations. It is cramped and offers little visibility, caution is essential. A path to the east runs along the coast and quickly get a glimpse of the Punta del Gomero. She's also particularly jagged. Then it is possible to reach Charco Verde and Charco De la Laja (see page 100).

The Paris daisy (*Argyranthemum frutescens*) brightens the steps of the stairs with its delicate yellow and white flower heads. If it reminds you something, it's normal, this native plant of the Canary Islands is massively used in horticulture, all around the world. Its Spanish name, margarita de las islas Canarias (Canary Island marguerite), reflects its origin.

The extra advice

Take the narrow path that goes east, slightly above the parking area exit, travel 50 m, stop and appreciate a magnificent view of the very indent cliffs and the Teide to the north.

 28°24'03.3"N 16°40'25.8"W

 Santa Catalina, 1.8 km away

 28°24'00.6" N 16°40'22.3" W

Charco Las Mujeres

Charco Las Mujeres

In a few lines

This relatively isolated place combines a high quality view of the ocean and a small charco in the middle of a wild coast.

The water point is a kind of aquarium, practical for beginning snorkelling. Perhaps the opportunity to observe particular animals, such as sea slugs (several species) and bearded fireworm (*Hermodice carunculata*).

Next to the car park, a former show platform now has lizards (*Gallotia galloti eisentrauti*) as its main actors. Wild canaries are sometimes perched in the surrounding trees, open your ears to hear their melodious song.

At the foot of the parking area stay the tiny Playa Las Mujeres.

Next to

Suitable for swimming directly in the ocean, Playa de las Arenas is reachable with a brief walk along the coast (about 400 m, to the east). The path takes place in a splendid landscaped setting. The beach also has its own parking slots.

 28°22'14.4" N 16°52'32.0" W

 28°22'10.6" N 16°52'30.3" W

 not served

 28°22'16.3" N 16°52'14.3" W (Playa de las Arenas)

Faro de Buenavista del Norte

Faro de Buenavista del Norte

In a few lines

Here is a lighthouse with a surprising design that makes the sound of the waves resonate in its hollow part. Built in 1990, it stands 41 m high and emits a powerful light that can be seen up to 37 km offshore. Along the coast to the west, the path quickly comes to an end and offers a glimpse of the imposing Teno massif looming on the horizon.
A walk along the coast is possible towards the east. Several charcos are located along the route and, shortly before Puertito de los Silos, an impressive blue whale skeleton is planted in the decor like a work of art.

On the way to the lighthouse, a short stop at Los Silos is appropriate. This authentic village aspires to calm. It only takes a few steps to discover its main assets: its bandstand which stands in the middle of the plaza de La Luz, the San Sebastián convent (with its rare openings) and the white church of Nuestra Señora. A few more steps reveal colourful adjoining facades sometimes accompanied by charming balconies or plants that take their ease in the roof.

Info

Did you know that each headlight has its light signature? The one in Buenavista del Norte lights up with 4 rapid flashes spaced at an interval of 11 seconds.

⊕ 28°23'28.0" N 16°50'11.2" W

 not served

P 28°23'28.0" N 16°50'11.2" W

Garachico

Garachico

In a few lines

Garachico had had its heyday. This small town then housed the island's most important commercial port.

At the beginning of the 18th century, a violent volcanic eruption put an end to this supremacy. Several lava flows crossed the town. One of them obstructed the cove which formed the natural harbour, making it unsuitable for merchant ships.

Nowadays, Garachico is no longer tormented by the Teide and its neighbours, serenity hovers in its charming alleys. On the seafront, a set of partially landscaped pools that make up the natural pools of El Caletón. Something to cool off or simply contemplate an atypical place. The historic centre is not lacking in elegance with, in particular, an important religious architectural heritage (several convents, churches and hermitages), especially around Plaza de la Libertad.

Further west, the Mirador el Emigrante offers a panorama to enjoy at a glance all the cachet of the small town, the Roque de Garachico offshore and the scar left by the eruption of 1706. Since the car park of the mirador, a discreet staircase descends between the rocks to lead to the Charco de Los Frailes, its turquoise waters, its crabs and its pretty fish.

Next to

If you are arriving from or departing from the south, your route will probably pass through the village of El Tanque. Don't miss a stop at Mirador Lomo Molino (28°21'33.9" N 16°47'08.9" W) which provides a magnificent view of the north coast of Tenerife.

  28°22'20.4" N 16°46'11.2" W

  28°22'18.6" N 16°46'04.7" W

 28°22'26.5" N 16°45'51.4" W

 28°22'29.5" N 16°45'49.2" W

 Piscina

Icod de los Vinos

Icod de los Vinos

In a few lines

Icod is a small town in the north that shares many similarities with its neighbours. Its main attraction is a magnificent Canary Islands dragon tree said to be millennial, although it would "only" be 800 years old. He is nonetheless the patriarch of his species. This sturdy tree is 17 m high with a circumference of about 20 m. It can be observed from the esplanade of the San Marcos church or from the park and del Drago interpretation centre (paying). A second specimen, almost as remarkable, is slightly cramped in the José Manuel Cabrera Square.

Plaza Andrés de Lorenzo Cáceres, widely planted with trees, hosts exotic species, including fig trees with remarkable trunks and aerial roots. It is urban around this square, Plaza La Constitución and the streets of San Sebastian and San Francisco that the most interesting points of the urban centre are articulated.

Next to

Unusual, on the heights of the town is the Cueva del Viento. At 18 kilometres, it is one of the longest lava tunnels in the world, dethroned only by a few colleagues from Hawaii. The Cueva del Viento can only be visited with a guide (www.cuevadelviento.net).

 28°22'01.2" N 16°43'15.3" W

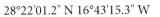 Estación Icod, 400 m away

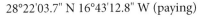 28°22'03.7" N 16°43'12.8" W (paying)

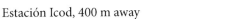 28°22'09.8" N 16°43'19.4" W (free)

La Orotava

favourite

La Orotava

In a few lines

La Orotava is arguably the prettiest town in Tenerife! In the very well-preserved streets of the old town there is a pleasant atmosphere, intertwined with the history and culture. Many religious buildings occupy the site, including the Nuestra Señora de la Conception church. It is pleasant to stroll through the colonial houses, such as the Casa de los Balcones, and along the cobbled streets.

Several parks can be visited, the best known is the Victoria Garden. This colourful terraced place was built in the 19th century by a French architect and commissioned by the Marquise de la Quinta Roja, so that her son could rest there in peace. The mausoleum, which dominates the park, however, has never been used. The church having finally accepted that the son of the marquise is buried in the family vault of the cemetery, despite his links with Freemasonry.

The main places to visit are located in the area delimited by the Plaza de San Francisco, the Nuestra Señora de la Conception church and the church of San Agustin, namely along Calle Carrera del Escultor Estévez and some neighbouring streets.

Next to

Slightly off-centre, nevertheless not to be missed, Los Lavaderos (28°23'12.0" N 16°31'32.3" W), are the old wash houses which illustrate a bygone era.

 28°23'21.7" N 16°31'29.8" W

 Ayuntamiento

 in the streets around the historic centre

 28°23'25.3" N 16°31'11.3" W

Miradors La Cruz de Juan Fernández

Miradors La Cruz de Juan Fernández

In a few lines

In Juan Fernández there are two main viewpoints. To embrace Teide, the north coast of Tenerife and the Atlantic Ocean at a glance, this is the place to go.

The first viewpoint (1), the top one, is extended by a small path (500 m round trip), to stretch your legs. The second (2) is located almost below, along the TF-163 which leads to El Pris. It offers a very similar view.

To complete the picture, with a view from the water level, it is possible to go to the car park of the port of El Pris (3) or to travel along the coast through then beyond this village (for a coastal walk, however, we recommend the Sendero El Sauzal instead, see page 124).

El Pris also benefits from a natural swimming pool consisting of a large pool by the ocean.

To take full advantage of the viewpoints, it is best to come when the sky is clear. Otherwise the landscape will be somewhat truncated. The show reaches its climax when the Teide is snow-capped.

Next to

About 8 km away, the Parque Los Lavaderos (28°28'41.0" N 16°26'18.7" W) offers, at its highest point, a similar panorama. It is therefore an alternative, where you can let yourself be surprised by a peaceful play of water between the basins of this old washhouse, in the shade of generous vegetation.

 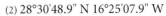 (2) 28°30'48.9" N 16°25'07.9" W

 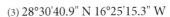 (3) 28°30'40.9" N 16°25'15.3" W

 (1) 28°30'46.6" N 16°25'04.4" W

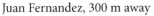 Juan Fernandez, 300 m away

 28°30'47.1" N 16°25'02.0" W (along the road)

Playa El Bollulo

Playa El Bollulo

In a few lines

Nestled between the jagged tips of Punta Romera and Punta del Fraile, El Bollulo is among the island's most renowned beaches. At high tide, the rounded shape of the rocks covering the upper portion of the beach creates a captivating relief, a phenomenon amplified under the late afternoon light. On the other hand, at low tide, the whole of this large expanse of black sand is revealed.

From the small access path, you can already enjoy an exceptional view of the coast and the ocean, before taking the stairs down to the shore (no reduced mobility access).

Generally rich in waves, Playa El Bollulo lends itself to swimming, but you have to be careful and watch the colour of the flag. Access is only open during surveillance hours, i.e. between 11 a.m. and 6 p.m. in summer (verano) and between 11 a.m. and 5 p.m. in winter (invierno).

The access road is very narrow, which makes the arrival or departure complicated during heavy traffic.

The extra advice

An alternative access is from the eastern end of Puerto de la Cruz. This adds 1.5 km on foot in the middle of the fincas (agricultural estates).

 28°25'03.8" N 16°31'10.8" W

 28°25'01.8" N 16°31'10.1" W (paying)

 El Rincón, 1.1 km away

 28°24'56.4" N 16°31'45.0" W (free), + 1.3 km

Puerto de la Cruz

Puerto de la Cruz

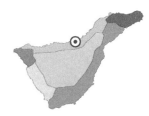

In a few lines

Formerly Puerto de la Cruz was only the port of La Orotava. When in 1706 Garachico was devastated by a lava flow, Puerto de la Cruz then took over and became the most important port of the island. Nowadays, this city is one of the main tourist stops on the north coast.

To appreciate the beauty of its still raw coastline and the contrast with the built one, you can, for example, take the Paseo de la Costa to the Mirador la Paz. There, to reach the lower part of the city, you have to follow Calle San Amaro, then the Escaleras Agata Christie and finally the longer Camino las Cabra. This neighbourhood is a reflection of the tourist flow it attracts, large hotels face bars and artificial bathing areas, including the famous Lago de Martiánez (paying). Further west is Playa San Telmo, a small urban beach in the heart of a rocky bay. Then, you can go up the alleys of the old town of Puerto de la Cruz and pass by the Plaza del Charco, a lively and friendly place where the locals relax. Its name comes from the fact that originally a charco existed in its centre.

Also discover the Sitio Liter Garden park or orchid garden (paying) which displays its rich floral collection in an intimate setting. In the same register, with more scope, the Orotava acclimatisation garden (paying) provides an immersion in the plant history of the island, as well as a variety of fascinating tropical flowers.

Dominating the city, the Taoro park offers a quality point of view: the Mirador de La Atalaya. The park surrounded by the Gran Hotel Taoro, established in 1890, a place of splendour from the beginning of the 20th century.

To cool off, there is Playa San Telmo and Playa del Castillo, in particular.

The extra advice

Puerto de la Cruz offers a wide range of services and is well located for exploring the north coast of Tenerife or for climbing to the Teide.

 28°24'58.1" N 16°32'50.6" W

 Puerto de la Cruz (main stop from outside)

 28°25'06.8" N 16°33'08.9" W

 28°24'55.6" N 16°32'50.5" W (often full)

Punta de Juan Centellas

Punta de Juan Centellas

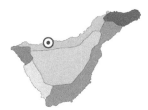

In a few lines

This point looks from the sky like a dinosaur foot embed in the ocean. The access path is quite perilous (it is better to take the one that passes in height than the one that runs along the edge). Once at the end of the trail, several natural formations with curious shapes are revealed, including an imposing petrified lava ridge that looks as if it was modelled by an artist.

The place dominates the Charco de Mareta surrounded by hostile rocks. This is a place to take time to watch the ocean do battle with the nearby cliffs. Several surrounding places are also called "playa", without being accessible and suitable for swimming.

Next to

Access to the water (at Charco de Mareta) is dangerous, for swimming prefer Playa de San Marcos (28°22'40.9" N 16°43'25.5" W), about 7 km by road direction west.

 28°23'40.1" N 16°41'38.2" W

 Hoya Meleque, 1.5 km away   28°23'28.2" N 16°41'32.5" W

Punta del Hidalgo

Punta del Hidalgo

In a few lines

The Punta del Hidalgo is the last flat area before the territory with marked relief of the rural park of Anaga. When you discover it for the first time, it gives the impression of an ultimate piece of civilisation before the unknown. To the east are sharp and jagged mountains that jut into the ocean, and to the west is a more subtle coastline, dressed in natural pools that unfold according to the lunar pull.

By joining the coast, the path successively runs along a wall with colourful graffiti and a small building, the Ermita San Juanito. The whole contributes to the singularity of this place. Further west is the impressive Faro de Punta del Hidalgo with its modern architecture. The path to get there passes in front of the comfortably furnished Charco de la Arena overlooked by a restaurant, then along other more rudimentary charcos.

For swimming, it is also interesting to refer to the Charco de la Furnia (28°34'14.1" N 16°20'00.0" W), which is located at the north-western limit of the urbanised area of Punta del Hidalgo. Its configuration, similar to a long breach in the lava, protects it from the waves. Access to water is via ladders.

Several hikes leave from Punta del Hidalgo to climb into the Ananga massif, notably at Mirador Aguaide, 600 metres above the ocean.

The extra advice

When you arrive, enjoy the panorama of the Mirador de la Punta Del Hidalgo. Avoid coming on weekends, as parking spaces are scarce in this popular place.

 28°34'16.5" N 16°19'04.0" W

 28°34'17.9" N 16°19'06.3" W

⊕ 28°34'42.0" N 16°19'16.2" W

 28°34'13.7" N 16°19'56.8" W (Charco la Furnia)

 Punta del Hidalgo, 50 m away

Sendero El Sauzal

favourite

Sendero El Sauzal

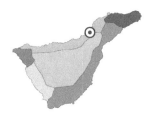

In a few lines

The coast of El Sauzal is an unmissable place in the north of Tenerife, wild and untamed, carrying its visitors away in an almost spiritual contemplation. However, this place was already occupied at the time of the *Guanches*, as evidenced by several dwelling caves. More recently, the area was squatted, with more than 400 illegal constructions, before the Canary Islands government decided to have them demolished. Thus, between 2007 and 2011, the buildings gradually disappeared in favour of a coastal path.

To the west, the tiny Ermita de Rojas and the view of El Esqueleto - the name given to the huge unfinished concrete and scrap structure of a 1970s housing project that sits enthroned on the cliff - creates an unrealistic canvas.

The Mirador de Las Breñas overlooks the entire coast of El Sauzal, so it is advisable to stop there. From the latter, it is possible to reach the Sendero El Sauzal on foot. It takes about 1 km and descends 200 m altitude.

The place is home to a variety of flora, including at least one Canary Islands dragon tree and a more discreet plant called "Pico de El Sauzal" (*Lotus maculates*). This endemic trefoil is in danger of extinction.

The extra advice

This place is beautiful, whether the sun is shining or it is raining. Equip yourself accordingly and go for it! A picnic spot with grills and water is available east of the car park.

 28°28'15.5" N 16°27'08.5" W

 28°28'21.0" N 16°26'43.1" W

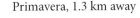 Primavera, 1.3 km away

 28°28'10.7" N 16°27'10.1" W

Region 5

Anaga massif

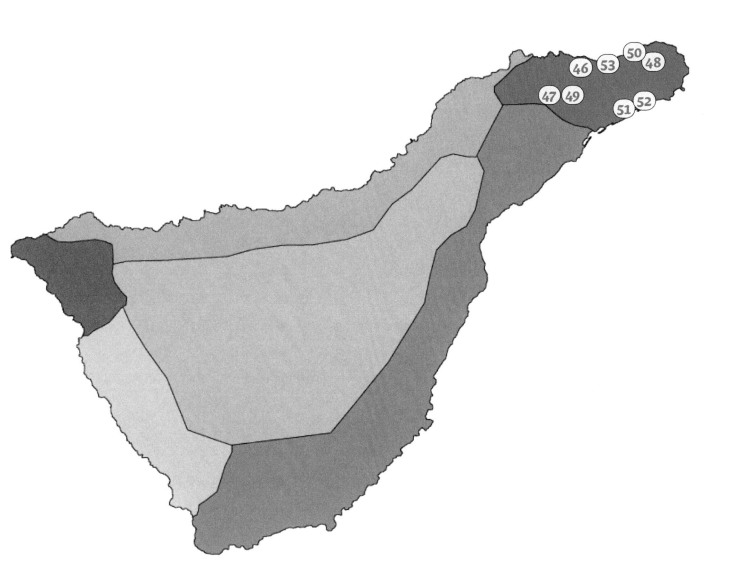

Barranco de Afur

favourite

p. 180

DESTINATION-TERRE.COM

Barranco de Afur

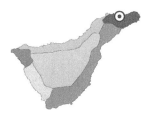

In a few lines

To experience the pleasure of exploring the Barranco de Afur, it is better to get up early, parking spaces are limited and the site very popular.

This easy hike offers discoveries all along the trail. The panoramas in particular are there, with a grand finish on the Playa del Tamadite. The Barranco de Afur is one of the few places where fresh water always flows. The vegetation is varied, this is observed especially in winter and early spring. The whole landscape is then green. In summer, it is a more arid version that can be contemplated. Arrived on the beach, beautiful cliffs command respect. The barranco is the territory of the goats that you may have the opportunity to see moving with ease in this chaotic relief.

At the beginning of the path, you will be able to observe a characteristic summit of Anaga, the Roque De Taborno, standing proudly like a tooth in the Alps.

The extra advice

Take your bathing suit, because if the access to the ocean is difficult because of the currents, the river forms a basin suitable for swimming, about 300 m before arriving on the beach.

 28°33'53.6" N 16°15'13.0" W

  Afur, 50 m away   28°33'19.7" N 16°14'53.5" W

Hija Cambada-Zapata

p. 181

Hija Cambada-Zapata

In a few lines

The hike starts in Cruz del Carmen. It is advisable to get there in the early morning, because being located at the start of several walking routes and located near La Laguna, this place is very popular. The proposed tour gives the opportunity to immerse yourself in the dense vegetation of the laurel forests. The concentration of foliage restricts the passage of light, especially when the understory is occupied by tree heather with multiple ramifications. The interplay of light and shadow and the tortuous silhouettes of the trunks thus create a landscape with a magical aspect and the trees forming real tunnels around the path in places.

Several birds appreciate the plant cover, in particular the African blue tit (*Cyanistes teneriffae*), with plumage similar to the blue tit, but darker.

There are several other options from Cruz del Carmen, including the Sendero de los Sendidos which heads south and leads to the Mirador del Llano de los Loros.

Next to

On the road to Hija Cambana, coming from La Laguna, stop at Mirador de Jardina (28°31'26.3" N 16°17'17.5" W) to admire the landscape that extends from the foot of the Anaga massif to the Teide.

 28°31'55.3" N 16°17'14.4" W

 Cruz del Carmen

 28°31'35.7" N 16°16'49.4" W

 28°31'52.3" N 16°16'47.9" W

Mirador Cabezo del Tejo

p. 182

Mirador Cabezo del Tejo

In a few lines

This viewpoint reveals one of the most beautiful panoramas of the Anaga massif. From there, the rugged terrain of the region is particularly easy to read. As a bonus, on a clear day, the Teide appears in the background.

To reach the viewpoint, you have to cross a magnificent ancient forest, wet, dense and rich in flora where ferns, mosses and epiphytic plants flourish.

This hike has the advantage of circumventing another route which requires authorisation (with limited and very busy places).

Along the way, the ambient humidity is conducive to small slug-like snails (*Insulivitrina lamarckii*), whose shell is reduced and under the skin.

At the end of the trail, you will certainly encounter Chaffinches of the Canary Islands subspecies (*Fringilla coelebs canariensis*). They have become accustomed to benefiting from a few scraps left by hikers.

Next to

For those who wish to take the neighbouring path, el sendero de El Pijaral (also called Ensillada), it is necessary to book in advance, see the relevant chapter (page 15).

 28°33'42.6" N 16°10'12.1" W

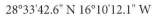

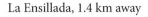 La Ensillada, 1.4 km away

 28°34'10.7" N 16°10'13.8" W

 28°33'30.4" N 16°10'13.1" W

Mirador Pico de Inglés

p. 183

DESTINATION-TERRE.COM

Mirador Pico de Inglés

In a few lines

The Mirador de Pico del Inglés offers a magnificent view of the Anaga massif. Easy to access, it is very popular, a real must in Tenerife. It allows for a modest loop through a low, mossy forest, where the trees seem to have bent to let you pass sovereignly on a small path in the middle of them.

The path ends up joining the Camino Viejo al Pico del Inglés. This astonishing scar made in the mountain is the route of an old road that leads to the east of the Anaga massif, now replaced by the TF-12. It is also a particularly photogenic and popular place. To immortalise it in complete privacy, be early!

Next to

Halfway between the viewpoint and the old road, the Sendero Monte Aguirre begins. To travel this path, it is necessary to book early, see our chapter page 15 on this subject.

 28°32'03.6" N 16°15'57.4" W

 Cruce Pico El Ingles, 500 m away

 28°31'57.1" N 16°15'49.7" W

 28°31'59.5" N 16°15'50.6" W

Playa Benijo

favourite

Playa Benijo

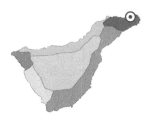

In a few lines

In the area there are three successive beaches (from west to east): Playa del Roque de las Bodegas (1), Playa de Almáciga (2) and Playa Benijo (3). The first is the most suitable for swimming. It owes its name to the colossal rock (roque) which delimits the cove and to the fact that the place was important for the local economy in the 17th and 18th centuries. Indeed, it is there that the wine of the surroundings (bodega meaning cellar) was loaded on the merchant ships.

Playa Benijo is magical! The wild and rough shores covered with large round stones, the sharp volcanic rocks, partially submerged offshore and whipped by powerful breaking waves make for a grand sight. It's the most secluded of the three beaches and the only one that involves some walking. To reach it, you have to walk along the coast from Playa de Almáciga (and park there) or take a staircase that starts below the lowest building in the hamlet of Benijo (28°34'28.8" N 16°11' 18.5" W). It is possible to park along the road directly behind the other two beaches.

The extra advice

To benefit from an expanse of black sand where to put a towel, it is better to favour the hours of low tide. The performance of the ocean with the glimmers of the end of the day is a must for an unchanging memory.

 (2) 28°34'19.3" N 16°11'34.0" W

 (3) 28°34'33.2" N 16°11'07.2" W

 (1) 28°34'09.4" N 16°12'17.7" W

 28°34'33.2" N 16°11'07.2" W

 Cruce de Almáciga, 1.7 km away

Playa de las Teresitas

Playa de las Teresitas

In a few lines

Near Santa Cruz, the Playa de las Teresitas looks like something out of a Caribbean postcard. Magnificent beach bordered by turquoise waters and covered with Saharan sand where a few palm trees provide some shade. It is the most imposing artificial beach on the island. It extends over more than a kilometre and required the transport of nearly 300,000 tons of sand from the Sahara.

Swimming and water games are greatly facilitated by a sea dyke that protects against the waves. This perfectly equipped setting contains several bather surveillance stations, as well as access for people with reduced mobility, showers, toilets, two volleyball courts, etc.

The beach is well served by public transport and has ample parking.

A stone's throw away is the multicoloured village of San Andrés, narrow houses on several levels and beautifully decorated balconies, there is no doubt that we are in the Canary Islands. The San Andrés Valley is also a place of *Guanches* archaeological remains.

Next to

It is pleasant to make a stopover in San Andrés which offers something to fill a little hollow after swimming or have a good meal.

  28°30'32.2" N 16°11'10.2" W

  28°30'32.0" N 16°11'14.0" W

Las Teresitas

Playa Las Gaviotas

Playa Las Gaviotas

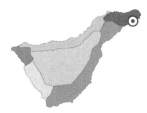

In a few lines

Nestled at the foot of the cliffs, this elegant strip of black sand is wilder than the previous one. With few services (only a bar), it nevertheless has lifeguards. Without a dyke or other structure of this type, the current and the waves are stronger there than on its large neighbour.
The beach is bordered by a car park that can be reached by following a winding road.

200 m to the north-east, a smaller beach, Playa Cueva del Agua, is worth a brief detour. It faces an imposing residential complex that follows the shape of the coast.

Next to

Along the way, stop at the Mirador de la Playa de las Teresitas! It offers a magnificent view of Playa Las Gaviotas, Playa de las Teresitas and San Andrés in a setting with rhythmic relief.

  28°30'48.1" N 16°10'33.0" W

  28°30'43.6" N 16°10'44.4" W

Playa Las Gaviotas, 1.2 km away

  28°30'49.6" N 16°10'29.6" W

Taganana-Tachero

p. 184

Taganana-Tachero

In a few lines

Taganana is a charming hamlet clinging to the steep and rocky slopes of the Anaga massif. This loop hike leads to the wild shores of Tachero Beach. It goes down by a small road which passes in front of the cultural centre and goes up by the Barranco de la Iglesia.

At the beginning of the walk, a detour allows you to appreciate a superb view of the coast and the ocean, for this you have to reach the cemetery from where a modest path starts. The latter crosses the bushes and climbs a mound.

The topography in the village of Taganana, as in many others in the region, limits the number of parking spaces. It is important to favour the bus or, sometimes, looking a while for a parking slot.

Next to

Arriving from the only access road, you can enjoy a view of Taganana and the surrounding hamlets, stopping at the Mirador Risco Amogoje.

⊕ 28°33'50.2" N 16°13'07.2" W

  Taganana, 100 m away

  28°33'45.5" N 16°13'10.8" W

  28°33'30.0" N 16°12'20.5" W

  28°33'32.9" N 16°12'59.4" W

Region 6

Centre (heights)

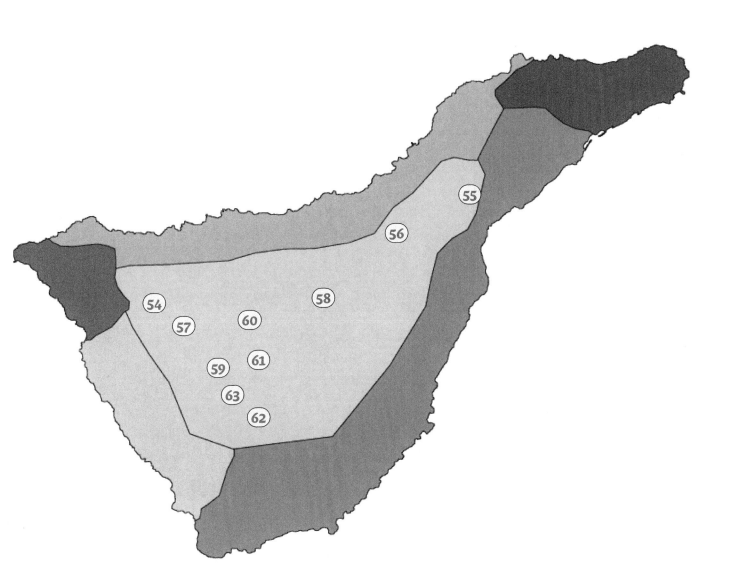

Chinyero

favourite

p. 185

Chinyero

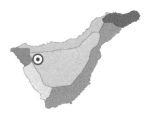

In a few lines

The Chinyero volcano is black and imposing. It culminates in 1560 m altitude. Its dark silhouette still bears the scars of its last eruption, just over a century ago, in the year 1909. This is what makes the landscape, relief and vegetation of this reserve so special.

The proposed loop allows you to go around it and takes visitors on a beautiful lava flow that is still raw. It is therefore a recent testimony to geological evolution on which we humbly tread.

There is no parking at the start of this hike, you will have to park at the Mirador de Los Poleos and take the opportunity to contemplate the island of La Gomera.

Access to the volcano is forbidden, respect this, it will only be more dazzling for the following hikers.

The extra advice

Do the hike in the afternoon, in order to stay in the evening at the Mirador de Los Poleos to admire the sunset. Provide warm clothes, as well as supplies. The sun sets in the ocean from early March to early October and behind La Gomera the balance of the year.

 28°17'39.6" N 16°45'26.2" W

 28°16'51.0" N 16°46'03.9" W

 not served

 28°17'04.6" N 16°45'45.0" W

Las Raíces

p. 186

Las Raíces

In a few lines

Las Raíces is an interesting place to discover the beauty of the Corona Forestal Natural Park and several marked paths leave from this recreational area.

The paths plunge into the heart of the pine forest of the Canary Islands. This is the opportunity to contemplate them closely, with their very long needles grouped in threes, while enjoying a glimpse of the ocean from time to time. Perhaps the occasion to admire a brightly coloured butterfly, the Macaronesian Vulcan (*Vanessa vulcania*), with bright orange bands on a black background, which only lives in the Canary Islands and Madeira.

Las Raíces is also a well-appointed recreation area with tables and grills available, so popular on weekends and holidays.

The extra advice

Picnic tables tend to be attractive to birds, so bring binoculars.

 28°25'06.7" N 16°22'52.9" W

 28°25'11.4" N 16°22'42.0" W

not served

Mirador de Chipeque

Mirador de Chipeque

In a few lines

This belvedere easily accessible by car offers one of the most beautiful views of the Teide. It is really essential to come there during your stay. This place is very popular at the end of the day. It must be said that this is one of the best spots for sunsets, even (or especially) with the sea of fog. It is therefore advisable to get there early enough to enjoy the show, with a good sitting spot. On the road that leads up to here (coming from La Laguna) there are several viewpoints with splendid panoramas. Teide and La Gomera are revealed each time from a different angle, but the result is always a pleasure for the eyes. We advise you to discover them in the following order: Mirador de Ortuno (1), Mirador de Chimague (2) and Mirador de Chipeque (3).

It is possible to park directly next to the viewpoints.

Next to

For those who have a little more time, extend the road to the Mirador de la Tarta (28°20'01.1" N 16°29'25.2" W). Another beautiful view of the Teide, but not only. A cut in the ground allows you to contemplate a series of the most aesthetic shades, resulting from the different layers of volcanic rocks.

 (1) 28°24'20.8" N 16°25'25.6" W

 not served

 (2) 28°22'23.2" N 16°27'34.6" W

 (3) 28°22'26.6" N 16°27'49.7" W

Montaña de Samara

favourite

p. 187

DESTINATION-TERRE.COM

Montaña de Samara

In a few lines

From the Mirador de Samara, several options are available to visitors, one of them begins with the climb to Montaña de Samara. The panorama is incredible, as always on this island! Once the modest summit is reached, we discover its crater as well as other volcanic cones scattered in the distance, including the Teide. The hike continues on a loop that goes around the Montaña de la Botija.

The ground is lined with needles in pale yellow hues and the whole is enhanced by the last soft green pines. The Corona Forestal stops at this altitude and the trees are only scattered, as if they had been carefully distributed by a painstaking landscaper.

Further south, along the TF-38, is the Pinar Chío recreational area, a beautiful picnic spot laid out in the shade of the lords of this forest. From there too, several hiking departures are possible.

The extra advice

This is a great location for star gazing. As elsewhere in altitude, the weather can change suddenly and the temperature cools quickly with the onset of the night. It is therefore important to provide layers in quantity to fully enjoy the show in good conditions.

  28°16'00.2" N 16°43'34.0" W

 28°16'00.2" N 16°43'34.0" W

  not served

 28°16'02.1" N 16°44'50.7" W (area of Pinar Chío)

Montaña del Cerrilar

favourite

p. 188

Montaña del Cerrilar

In a few lines

The path, named "loop of the black sands", goes around the Montaña del Cerrilar. The terrain is a succession of variants of ochre and brown, from light to dark, with many bushes that emphasise the topography. Some passages once again reveal the Teide in its most beautiful aspect, while others run along steep-sided furrows filled with finely ground and sooty-black volcanic rock.

After crossing two thirds of the loop, the origin of its name becomes obvious. Everything appears beautifully dark. Anthracite dominates as one treads on the lava reduced to small pieces. Have you ever walked into a giant bowl of crispy cereal? That's probably what it should look like. However, it is not recommended to taste it.

In the early morning, the "pimelia del Teide" (*Pimelia ascendens*) is very common in places. It is a black beetle with nocturnal habits that is only found on the heights of Tenerife.

Next to

The El Portillo visitor centre is next door. Here you can discover the birth of Tenerife and find valuable information about the national park, its fauna and flora. The centre also has a botanical garden, accessible at all times.

28°17'41.5" N 16°33'12.9" W

El Teide - El Portillo, 400 m away

P 28°18'13.2" N 16°34'00.8" W

Museo ethno Juan Évora

p. 189

DESTINATION-TERRE.COM

Museo ethno Juan Évora

In a few lines

From the Museo Etnográfico Juan Évora, two hikes are offered. The first goes north-west. It crosses an impressive lava flow dating from 1798. Although more than 100 years older than that of Chinyero (see page 146), it has lost none of its darkness. It must be said that it comes from the last eruption in the Caldera de las Cañadas, where the climate is particularly harsh. The approximately 4 km long lava tongue can easily be seen in aerial photos. The site is in the shade for a long time, so it is necessary to provide clothes accordingly.

The second hike begins south. It descends rapidly into the Barranco de Erques, in the middle of the Canary pines, where the luckiest and most attentive can observe the Tenerife blue chaffinch (*Fringilla teydea*). The large and beautiful Tenerife bugloss (*Echium wildpretii*) also lives here. It's an endemic and emblematic flower, high in colour and size. Flowering, red, takes place mainly between May and June.

Both hikes are quite short and can therefore be done on the same day.

Next to

As the locality name indicates, there is an ethnographic museum (free). This is an exhibition about the living conditions of Juan Évora, the last inhabitant of the national park. Please note that the car park is closed at the same time as the museum. For more flexibility on the schedule, parking in Boca Tauce is a good alternative.

 28°13'25.0" N 16°41'42.7" W

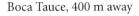 Boca Tauce, 400 m away

 28°12'45.7" N 16°40'52.3" W

 28°12'50.9" N 16°40'42.1" W

Pico del Teide

Pico del Teide

In a few lines

Pico del Teide, the roof of Spain culminates at 3718 m altitude. If we consider its submerged part, it is the third-highest volcanic formation in the world. This majestic cone sits enthroned over Tenerife, you can admire it from a thousand places without ever getting tired of it. For some, it is the very essence of travel on this island. To climb it, two options are possible, the first, a particularly difficult hike starting from Montaña Blanca, which will have to be carefully organised. Ideally plan a stopover at the Altavista refuge in order to have time to enjoy this experience.

The second option, more physically accessible, but also more expensive, is to take the cable car which stops at an altitude of 170 m below the highest point. From here, the watchtower already offers a masterful view. To reach the crater and complete the last 600 metres, prior authorisation must be issued by the Teide National Park. All the information on this subject and also on the reservation of the cable car can be found in the dedicated chapter (page 15). At the foot of Teide is Montaña Blanca, whose light colour seen from the sky is due to the type of phonolitic lava that covers it. During this type of explosive eruption, lapilli (pumice stones) is thrown high into the air, which is why they now cover a large portion of the Caldera de las Cañadas.

The Pico Viejo, whose impressive 800 m diameter crater attracts hikers, is easily reached from the arrival of the cable car. Other paths, more physically involved, starting from neighbouring viewpoints.

Next to

The Mirador Minas de San José is a desert stage at the foot of Teide. There, the sand and the lapilli form clear and crispy dunes. An interesting place to observe the caldera.

 28°16'20.2" N 16°38'32.9" W

 28°15'55.1" N 16°35'21.1" W

 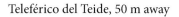 Teleférico del Teide, 50 m away

 28°15'19.9" N 16°37'30.4" W

Roques de Garcia

favourite

p. 190

Roques de Garcia

In a few lines

An essential place in Tenerife, this excursion goes around the Roques de García. Along the trail, emblematic rocks follow one another, such as Roques de Cinchado, El Torrotito, El Burro or Roques Blancos. Their amusing silhouettes will tickle the imagination of some people. Sometimes we see an animal, a familiar face, etc. Once the northern end is crossed, where the imposing stone monsters stop, the descent begins on a bed of frozen lava. The grandeur of the natural monuments that surrounds this place is very impressive and somewhat destabilising. At the lowest point, the path arrives at the foot of a rock formation over 100 m high: La Catedral. This volcanic chimney is a pile of gradually consolidated lava as it emerged into the open air.

Tenerife lizards (*Gallotia galloti galloti*) are visible throughout the loop and are attracted to picnic scents.

The car park is quickly taken over, but often visitors only stop to take a few photos, without hiking, with a little patience you will find a place.

The place is also fabulous for contemplating the stars with the silhouettes of Teide and Roque Cinchado.

Info

The Roque Cinchado is so iconic that it appeared on 1000 Spanish pesetas banknotes in the 1980s, long before the euro was launched.

 28°13'35.1" N 16°38'05.2" W

  28°19'05.5" N 16°22'43.2" W

 Parador del Teide, 400 m away

  28°17'54.2" N 16°22'16.5" W

Vilaflor de Chasna

p. 191

Vilaflor de Chasna

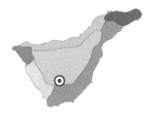

In a few lines

Vilaflor is the city of heights. This town with typical Canarian charm is located on the edge of the Corona Forestal natural park. It is known for its wine and its elegant historic houses. It is a stopover of choice on the Teide route or for a day.

To contemplate its architecture, it is better to take a few more altitude by going to the Ermita de San Roque. From Vilaflor, a path leads to Pino Enano ("dwarf" pine), a tree with a particular silhouette. In the distance, you will be able to see the sombrero of Chasna, a large circular and flat rock on it. A few picnic tables are available. At the start of the path, towards the football field, there are also covered tables.

Next to

Along the TF-21 road, a few switchbacks above Vilaflor, stands Pino Gordo. Literally "fat pine", this is the name given to the largest Canary Island pine of Tenerife. Majestic, this tree reaches 45 m in height for a circumference of 10 m. It should have been between 700 and 800 years old. Next to it is another imposing pine, the Pino de las dos Pernadas.

 28°09'33.5" N 16°38'11.8" W

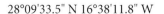 Vilaflor Centro

 28°09'54.9" N 16°38'11.5" W (Pino Gordo)

 28°09'37.6" N 16°38'13.4" W

Zona Recreativa Las Lajas

p. 192

Zona Recreativa Las Lajas

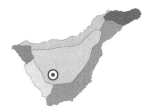

In a few lines

This welcoming picnic spot equipped with tables and stone barbecues brings together the inhabitants of Tenerife in large numbers once the week has come to an end. Las Lajas is located in a setting of Canary Island pines in the heart of the Corona Forestal natural park, where shade and coolness are very popular. Often battling with clouds, the place is particularly graceful as it gently peeks out from clouds that form a sea of fog, at sunset.
It is also the starting point for a pleasant hike with an unforgettable view of the Caldera de las Cañadas.

The extra advice

Between the pines and around the picnic tables prowl many forest birds: Tenerife blue chaffinch, African blue tit, common kestrel... Equip yourself with binoculars.

 28°11'24.2" N 16°39'57.3" W

 Las Lajas, 100 m away   **P** 28°11'26.4" N 16°39'55.9" W

Hike - Arco de Tajao

↔ 3.4 km ↗ 120 m ↘ 120 m 🕐 1 h 20 ⛰ 0-50 m

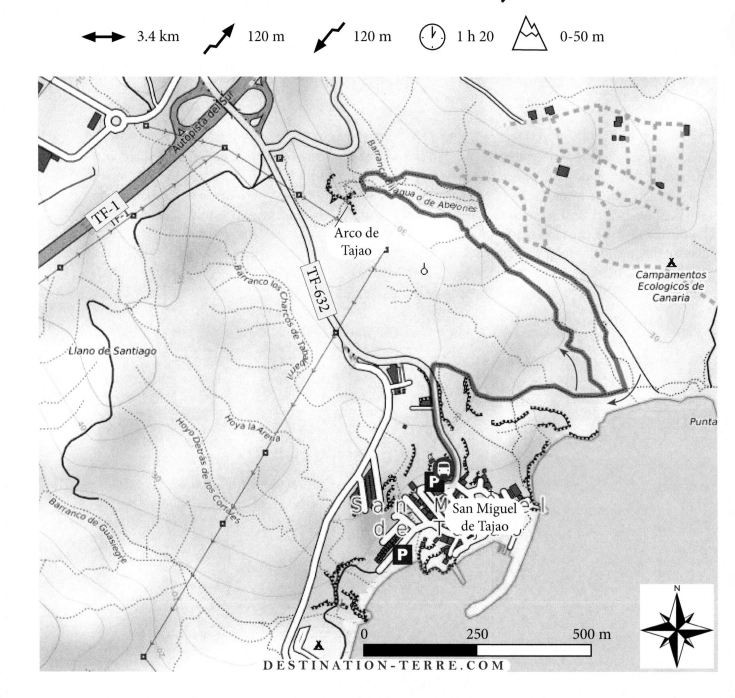

TF-1

TF-1

Autopista del Sur

Barranco de Jagua o de Abejones

Arco de
Tajao

TF-632

Barranco los Charcos de Tabaibl...

Llano de Santiago

Hoya la Arena

Hoyo Detrás de los Cortijos

Barranco de Guasiegre

Campamentos
Ecologicos de
Canaria

Punta

San Miguel
de Tajao

San Miguel de Tajao

0   250   500 m

N

DESTINATION-TERRE.COM

Hike - Los Derriscaderos

↔ 7.4 km ⬈ 170 m ⬊ 170 m ⏱ 2 h 45 ⛰ 100-250 m

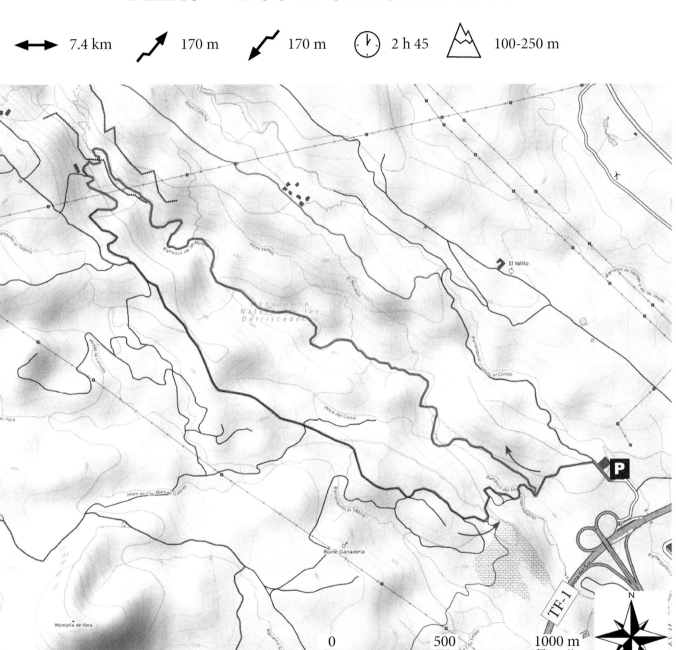

Hike - Malpaís de Güímar

↔ 8 km   ↗ 130 m   ↘ 130 m   🕐 2h50   ⛰ 0-100 m

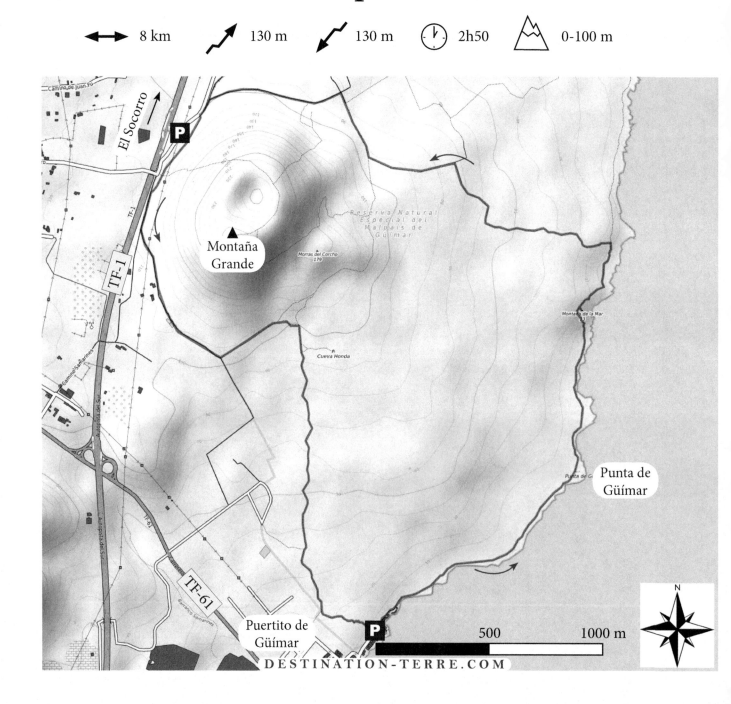

El Socorro

P

TF-1

TF-1

Camino Sañarmes

Autopista del Sur

Camino de Juan Fe

▲ Montaña Grande

Reserva Natural Especial del Malpaís de Güímar

Morras del Corcho 179

Cueva Honda

Montaña de la Mar

Punta de Güímar

TF-61

Barranco Sañarmes

Autopista del Sur

Puertito de Güímar

P

500   1000 m

N

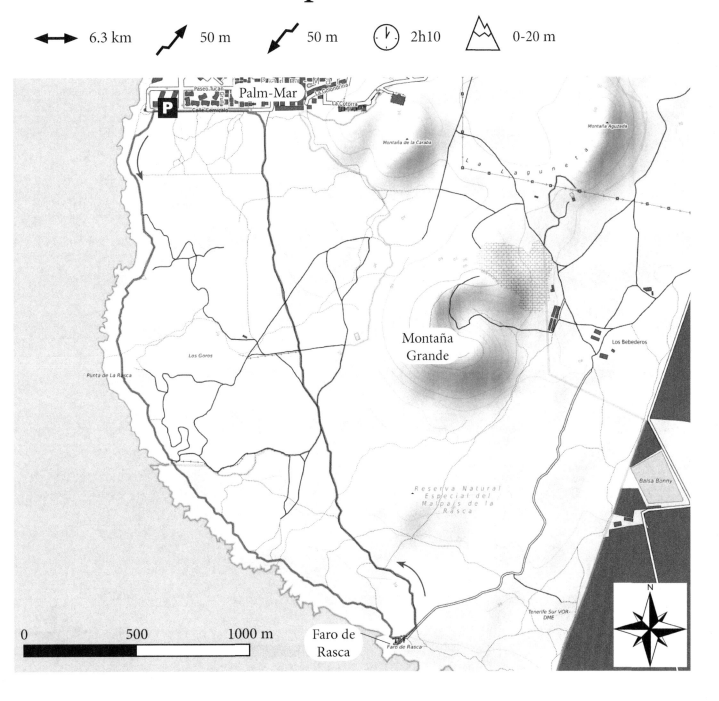

6.3 km 50 m 50 m 2h10 0-20 m

Palm-Mar

Paseo Tucán
Calle Cenícalo
La Golondrina
La Cotorra

Montaña de la Caraba

Montaña Aguazada

La Laguneta

Montaña
Grande

Los Bebederos

Los Goros

Punta de La Rasca

Reserva Natural
Especial del
Malpaís de la
Rasca

Balsa Bonny

Faro de
Rasca

Faro de Rasca

Tenerife Sur VOR-
DME

0   500   1000 m

N

Hike - Montaña Amarilla

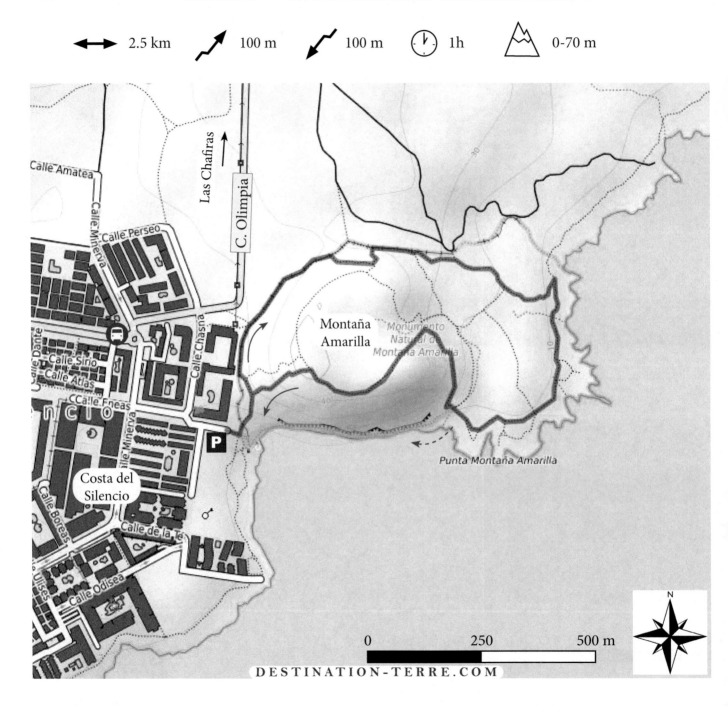

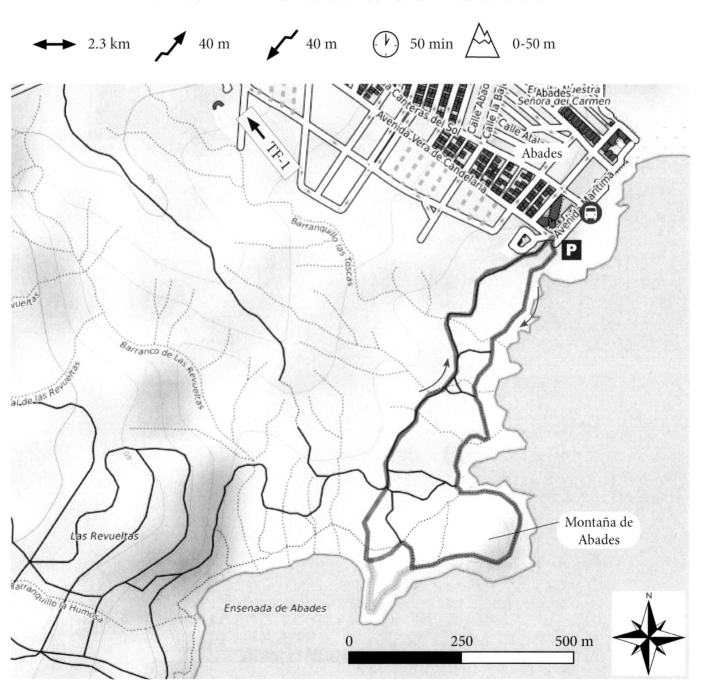

2.3 km 40 m 40 m 50 min 0-50 m

TF-1

Abades

Montaña de
Abades

Las Revueltas

Ensenada de Abades

0   250   500 m

Hike - Montaña de Guaza

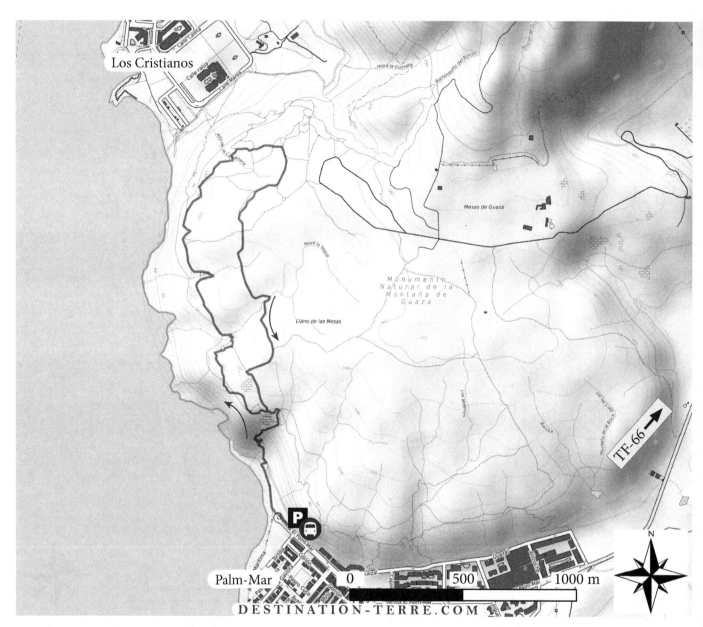

↔ 5 km   ↗ 170 m   ↘ 170 m   🕐 2h   ⛰ 0-120m

Los Cristianos

Hoya la Guirrela

Barranquillo del Buccon

Mesas de Guaza

Hoya la Yegua

Monumento Natural de la Montaña de Guaza

Llano de las Mesas

TF-66

Palm-Mar

0   500   1000 m

DESTINATION-TERRE.COM

4.3 km   150 m   150 m   1h45   0-100 m

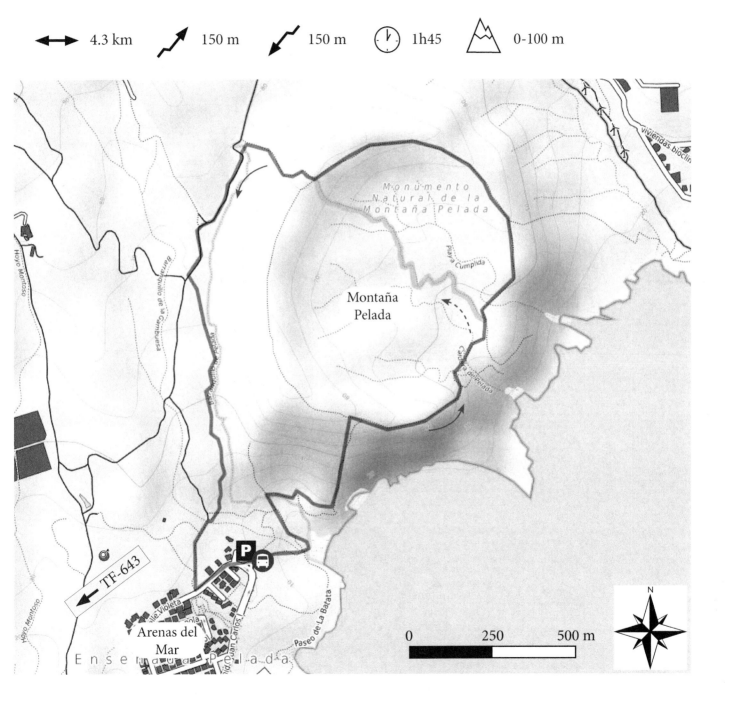

Monumento
Natural de la
Montaña Pelada

playa Cumplida

Montaña
Pelada

Caldera de Pelada

Hoyo Montoso

Barranquillo de la Gambuesa

viviendas bioclin

P

TF-643

Calle Violeta

Avenida Juan Carlos I

Paseo de La Batata

Arenas del
Mar

Ensenada Pelada

Hoyo Montoso

0   250   500 m

N

Hike - Montaña Roja

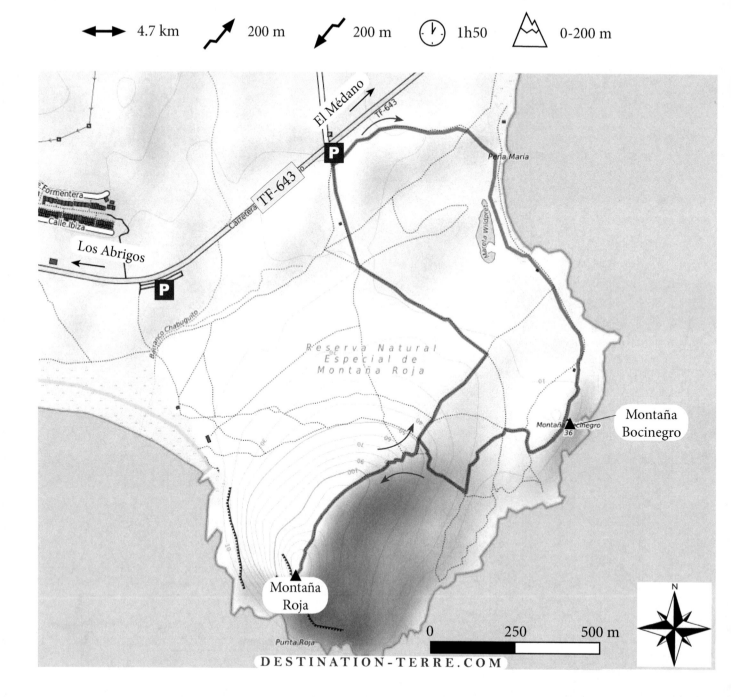

4.7 km   200 m   200 m   1h50   0-200 m

El Médano

TF-643

Peña María

Carretera TF-643

Matela Wildpret

Los Abrigos

Formentera

Calle Ibiza

Barranco Chabuguito

R e s e r v a N a t u r a l
E s p e c i a l d e
M o n t a ñ a R o j a

Montaña Bocinegro
36

Montaña
Bocinegro

Montaña
Roja

Punta Roja

0   250   500 m

N

Hike - Roque de Jama

↔ 2.2 km   ↗ 150 m   ↙ 150 m   🕐 1 h 30   ⛰ 600-800 m

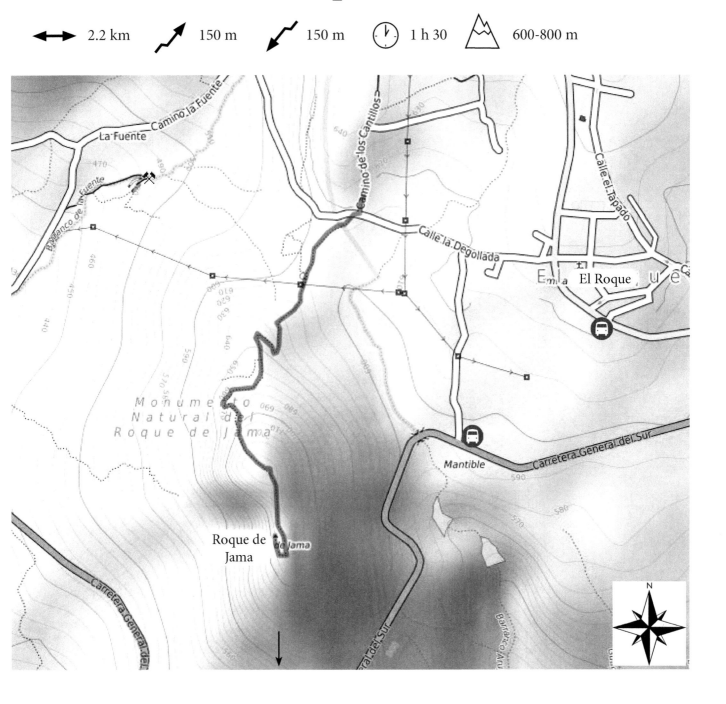

Hike - Masca-Roque de la Fortaleza

↔ 6 km   ↗ 270 m   ↘ 270 m   🕐 3h   ⛰ 700-800 m

Buenavista del Norte

TF-436

Mirador La Cruz de Hilda

La Bica

El Turrón

Nuestra Señora de la Concepción

Masca

Santiago del Teide

Pico Yeye

Roque de Fortaleza

Barranquera Honda

Barranco de Juan Lopez

Barranco del Retamal

Hoya las Tabaibas

Cumbres de Bolico

Cumbre de Masca

Las Pilas

0   250   1000 m

N

Hike - Montaña Bilma

7.6 km   300 m   300 m   3h   900-1300m

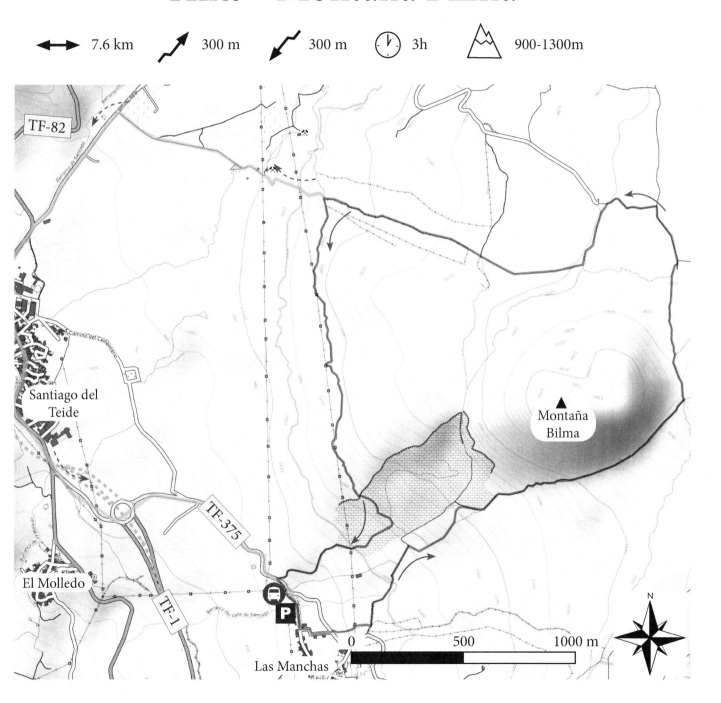

Hike - Monte del Agua-Erjos

↔ 6 km   ⬈ 250 m   ⬊ 250 m   🕐 2h30   ⛰ 1000-1200 m

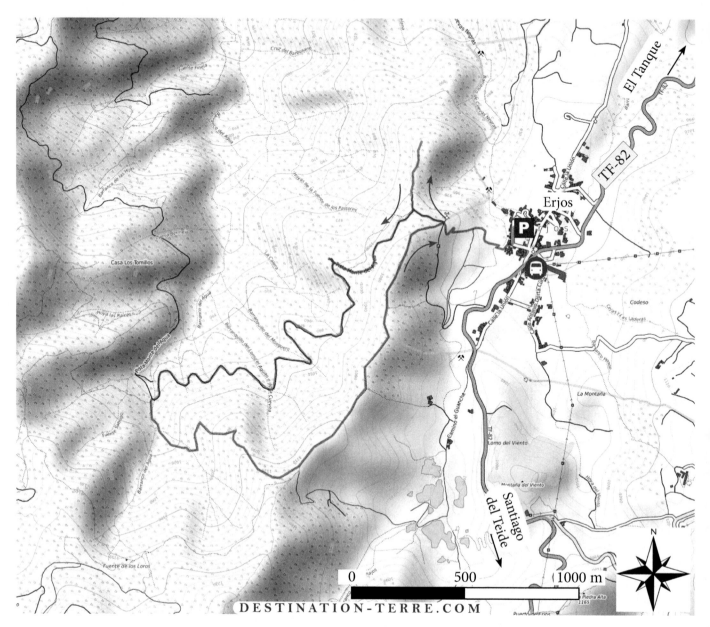

DESTINATION-TERRE.COM

Hike - Barranco de Ruiz

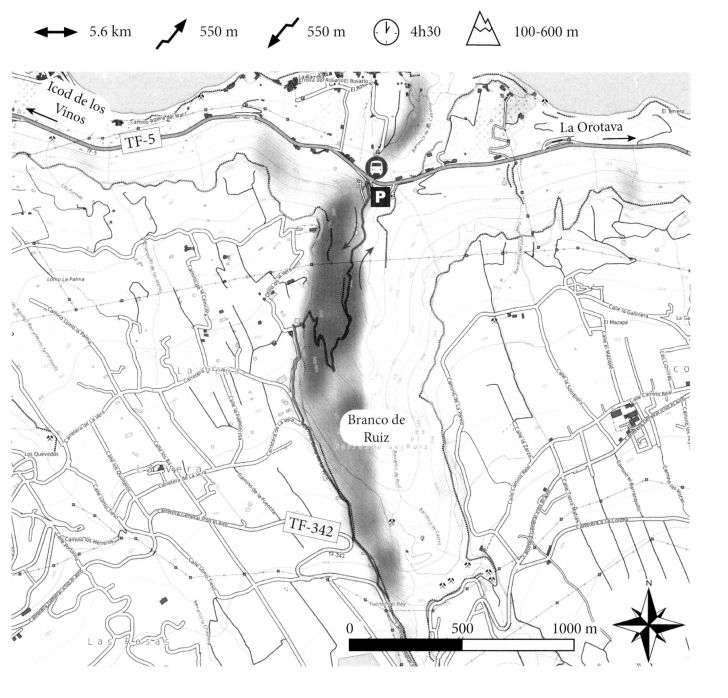

Hike - Barranco de Afur

↔ 5.3 km ↗ 220 m ↘ 220 m 🕐 2h15 ⛰ 0-250m

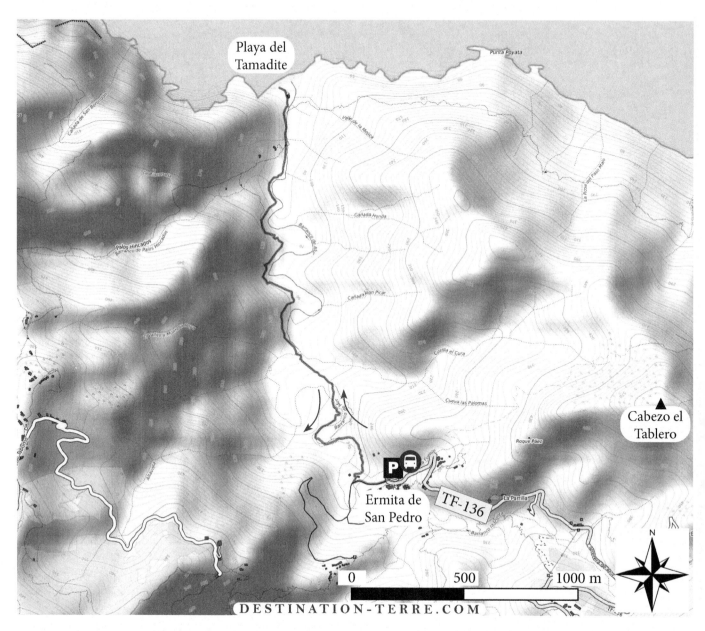

Playa del Tamadite

Punta Poyata

Valle de la Monica

Cañada de San Bartolomé

Palos Hincados
Barranco de Palos Hincados

Barranco de Afur

Cañada Honda

La Rosa del Pozo Muelo

El Valle y el Mondalejo

Cañada Juan Picar

Cuesta el Cura

Cueva las Palomas

Roque Páez

Cabezo el Tablero

P 🚌

Ermita de San Pedro

La Parrilla

TF-136

Barranco de Afur

0   500   1000 m

N

Hike - Hija Cambada-Zapata

↔ 5 km   ↗ 200 m   ↘ 200 m   🕐 2h   ⛰ 800-1000 m

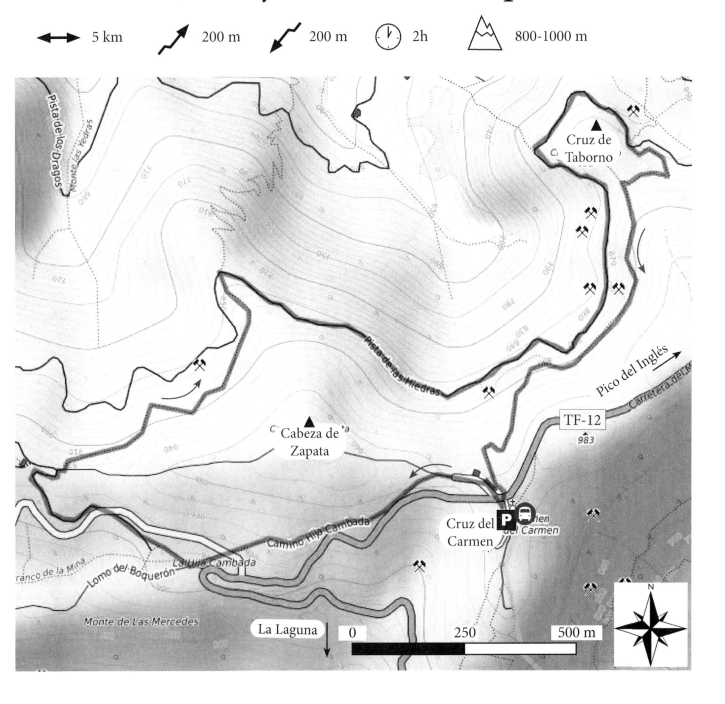

Hike - Mirador Cabezo del Tejo

↔ 6 km   ↗ 200 m   ↘ 200 m   🕐 2h20   ⛰ 700-850 m

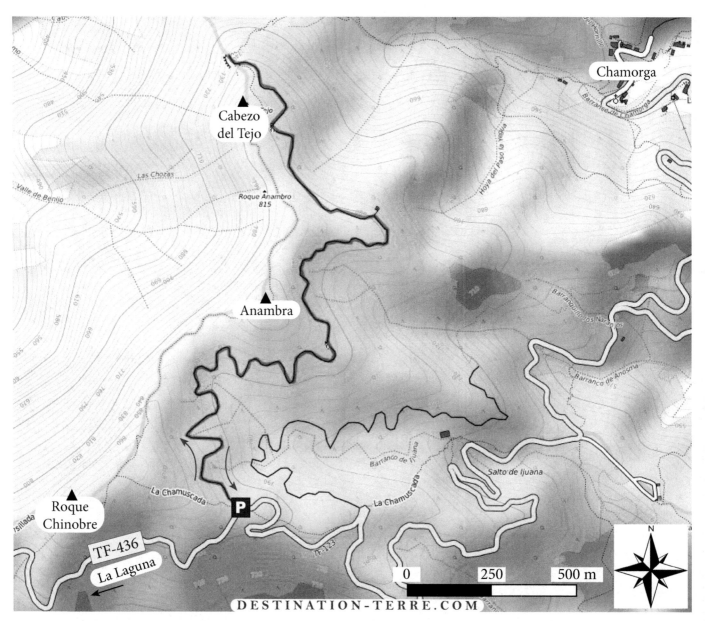

Hike - Mirador Pico de Inglés

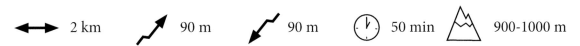

↔ 2 km   ↗ 90 m   ↘ 90 m   ⏱ 50 min   ⛰ 900-1000 m

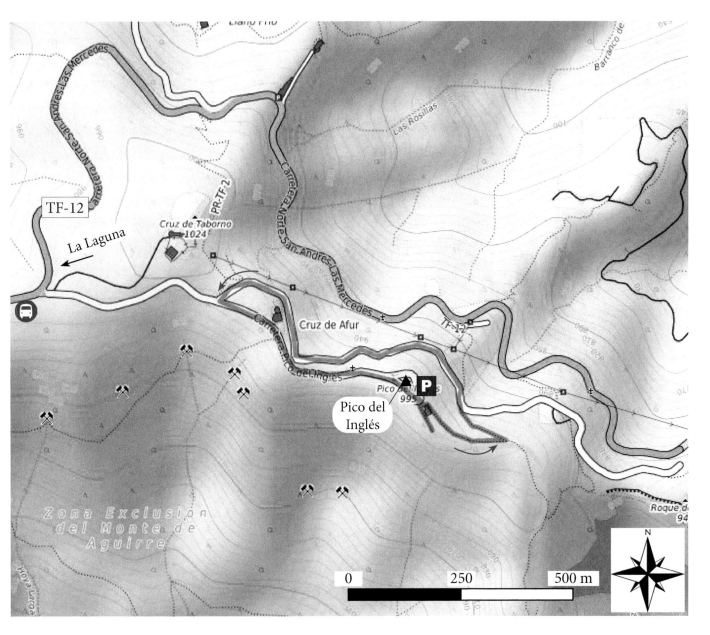

Hike - Taganana-Tachero

3.5 km   170 m   170 m   1h30   0-200 m

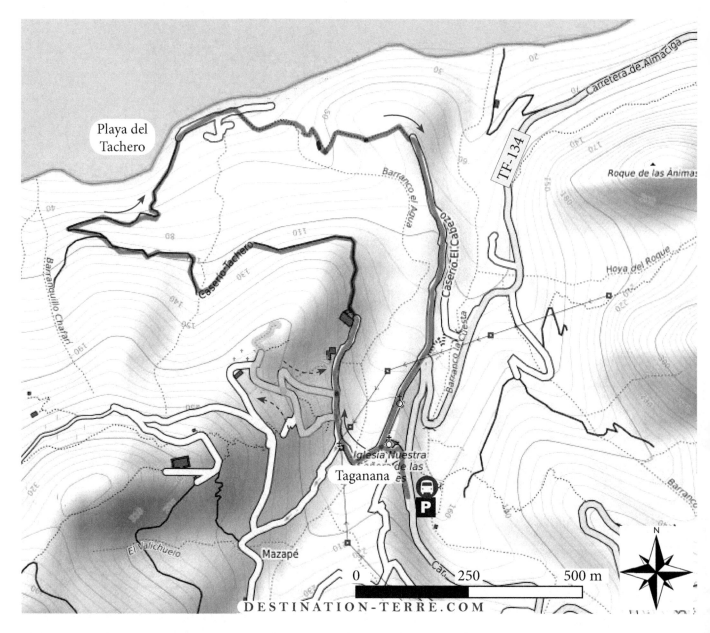

Playa del Tachero

Carretera de Almaciga

Roque de las Ánimas

Barranco el Agua

TF-134

Caserío Tachero

Caserío El Cabe

Barranco la Cuesta

Hoya del Roque

Iglesia Nuestra de las es

Taganana

Mazapé

El Valichuelo

0   250   500 m

N

DESTINATION-TERRE.COM

Hike - Chinyero

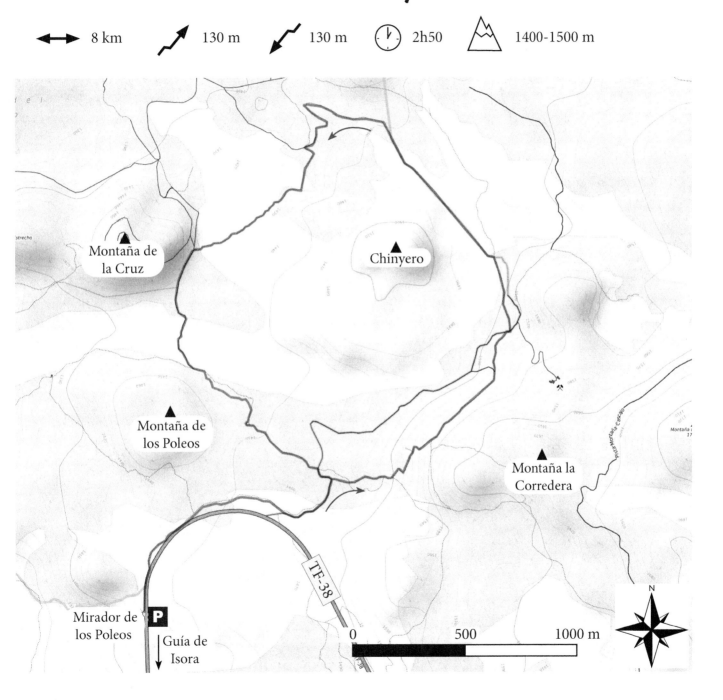

↔ 8 km   ↗ 130 m   ↙ 130 m   🕐 2h50   ⛰ 1400-1500 m

Montaña de la Cruz

Chinyero

Montaña de los Poleos

Montaña la Corredera

TF-38

Mirador de los Poleos

P

Guía de Isora

0   500   1000 m

N

Hike - Las Raíces

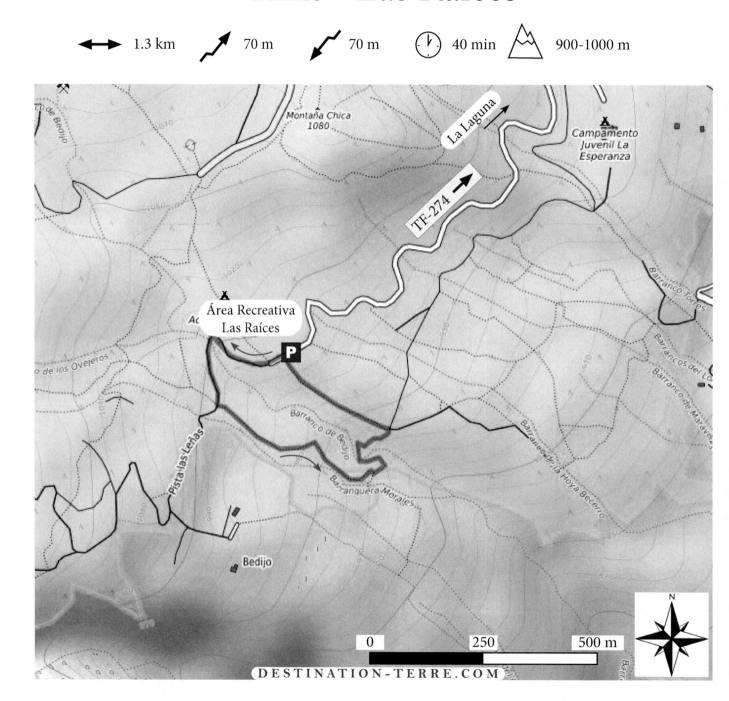

↔ 1.3 km   ↗ 70 m   ↘ 70 m   🕐 40 min   ⛰ 900-1000 m

Montaña Chica 1080

La Laguna

TF-274

Campamento Juvenil La Esperanza

Área Recreativa Las Raíces

P

Barranco de Bedijo

Pista las Leñas

Barranquera Morales

Barranco de la Hoya Becerro

Bedija

0   250   500 m

N

DESTINATION-TERRE.COM

Hike - Montaña de Samara

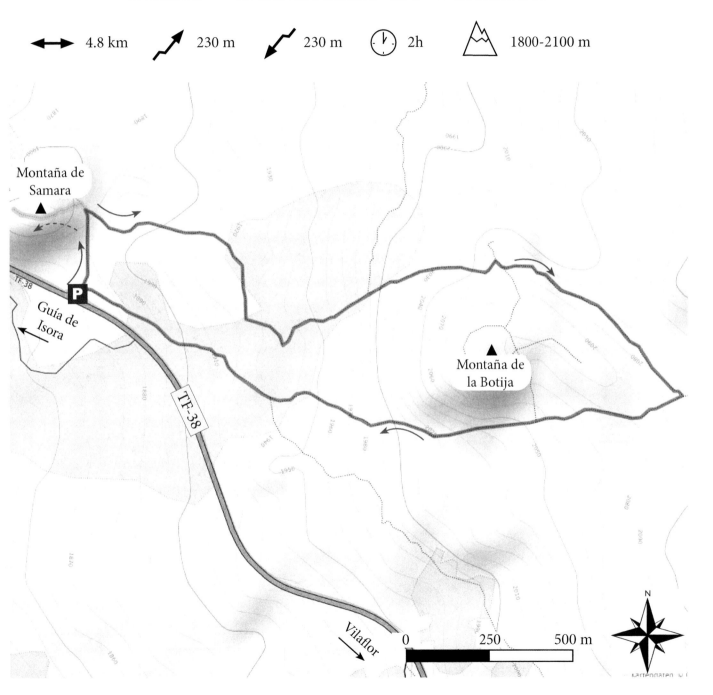

↔ 4.8 km   ↗ 230 m   ↘ 230 m   🕐 2h   ⛰ 1800-2100 m

Montaña de Samara ▲

TF-38

P

Guía de Isora

TF-38

Vilaflor

Montaña de la Botija ▲

0   250   500 m

N

Hike - Montaña del Cerrilar

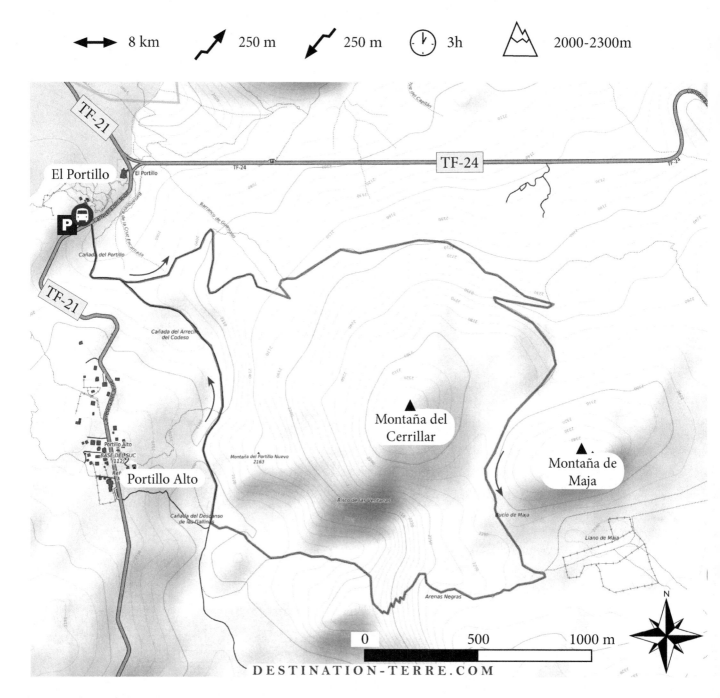

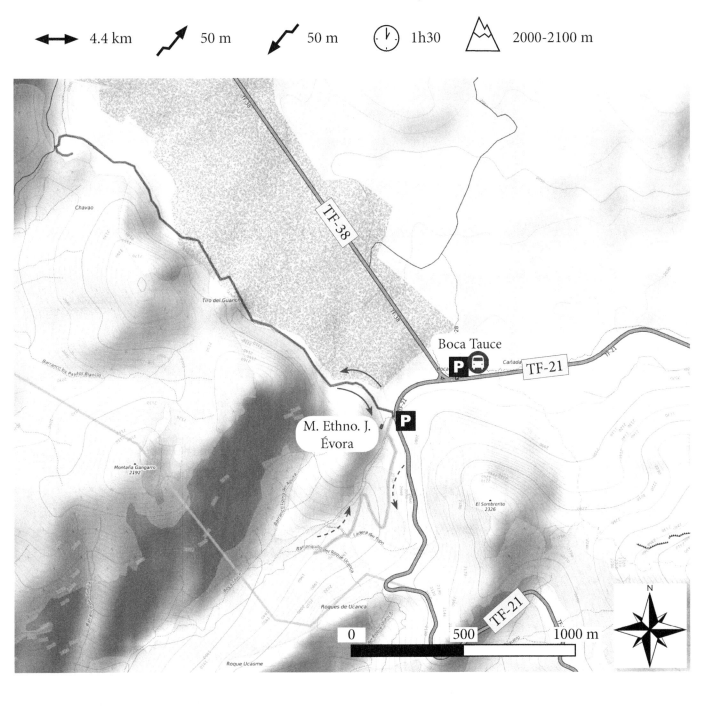

Hike - Roques de Garcia

↔ 3.7 km   ↗ 150 m   ↘ 150 m   🕐 2h   ⛰ 2000-2200 m

La Laguna

TF-21

TF-21

Parador de
Cañadas del
Teide

Félix Méndez

Roque ▲
Cinchado   chado

La Catedral ▲
ral

P

Vilaflor

N

0   250   500 m

5.5 km   250 m   250 m   2h20   1400-1700 m

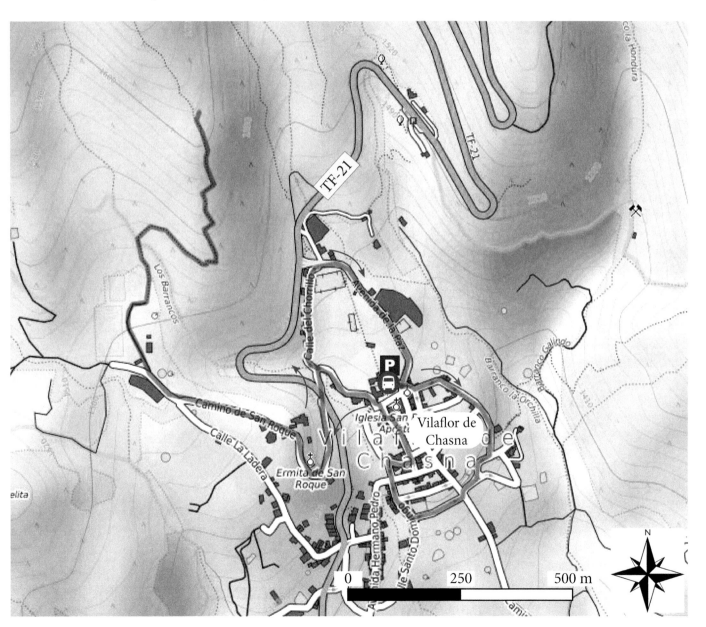

Hike - Zona Recreativa Las Lajas

↔ 6.5 km ⤴ 400 m ⤵ 400 m 🕐 3h ⛰ 2100-2500 m

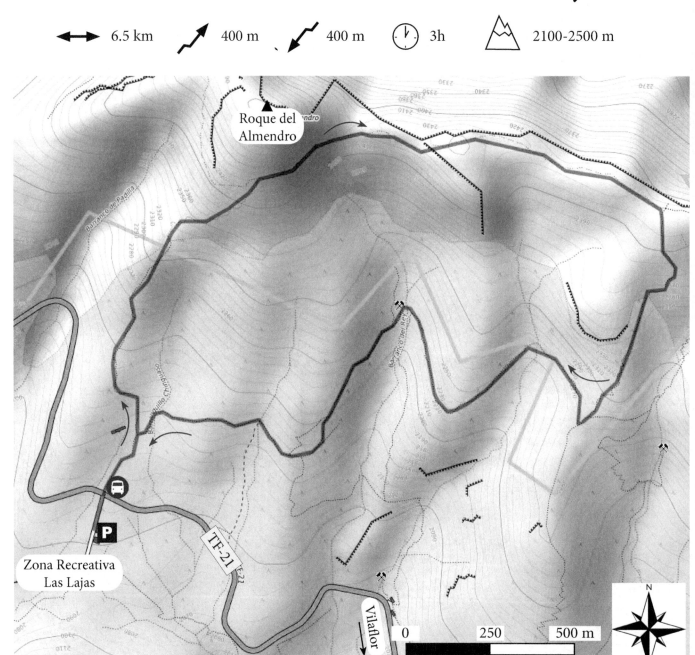

Roque del Almendro

Barranco de Padilla

Barranquillo Chinguaro

Barranco del Rey

Zona Recreativa Las Lajas

P

TF-21

Vilaflor

0 250 500 m

N

Copyrights

ISBN: 9798444186534

Printed in Great Britain
by Amazon

24143078R00110